Genoa
Nice
Monaco
Cannes
Raphael
St.Tropez
ELBA
Bastia
Calvi
CORSICA
Ajaccio
Porto Vecchio
Bonifacio
SARDINIA

French Mediterranean Harbours

Nautical
Mediterranean Harbours & Anchorages series

Philip Bristow
French Mediterranean Harbours

Nautical Publishing Company Limited

© Philip Bristow 1974

First published in Great Britain by
Nautical Publishing Company Limited
Lymington, Hampshire SO4 9BA
in association with
George G. Harrap & Company Limited
182-184 High Holborn, London WC1V 7AX

ISBN 0 245 51001 X

By the same author
Bristow's Book of Yachts
Through the French Canals
Through the Belgian Canals
Through the Dutch Canals
Down the Spanish Coast

*Despite every effort to ensure that information given in this
book is accurate and up-to-date, it is regretted that neither author
nor publisher can accept responsibility for errors or omissions.*

Filmset and printed in Great Britain by
BAS Printers Limited, Wallop, Hampshire

To Emma and Fred

Acknowledgements

I am indebted to many Departments of the French Government for the facts and figures that they have kindly made available to me; to the many officials in Capitainerie and Syndicat d'Initiative who have patiently dealt with my requests for information; and particularly to Pauline Hallam, Director of Public Relations, French Government Tourist Office for her kindness and help.

Contents

Introduction by Pauline Hallam

1. The Yachtsman's Mecca   11
2. Suitable and Unsuitable Boats   35
3. Equipment   43
4. Cost of Living   48
5. Weather—and Miscellaneous Items   54
6. Harbours West of the Rhône   58
7. Harbours East of the Rhône   88
8. Corsica   152

Index   173

Introduction
by
P. HALLAM,
Director of Public Relations
FRENCH GOVERNMENT TOURIST OFFICE   Piccadilly,
LONDON

From the glamorous days of the 18th and 19th centuries right up to the stunning times of pop stars and topless St. Tropez, the South of France has always been the number one playground of the world's adults—particularly if they happened to be millionaires on board their yachts.

For the visitor of the seventies, there would appear to be little more to discover. And yet . . .

On the fabled Riviera-Côte d'Azur, new marinas and traditional ports offer moorings to craft of all sizes and there is no need to have a fortune to enjoy the pleasures of the coast.

Farther west, in under ten years, the coastline has been developed into one of the finest yachting and holiday centres of the Mediterranean, the Languedoc-Roussillon. Stretching from La Grande Motte to the foothills of the Pyrenees, although steeped in histories, it had been one of the forgotten areas of France until 1964.

And across the water, the romantic Scented Isle of Corsica. Here, too, harbours are being enlarged and marinas built to take craft—with great care not to spoil the beauty of the island.

With such a wealth of choice, how to decide where to drop anchor? Philip Bristow's book will provide an invaluable guide with its accurate charts and excellent detailed information.

Cannes—the most fabulous yachting port in the world   Photo: Baconnet—Cannes

Monaco is surely the grandest yacht harbour of all. Photo: Guy Ventouillac

1 The Yachtsman's Mecca

It seems to be only a few years ago that we used to ghost up into the Golfe de Frejus, half closing our eyes, imagining that we were coaxing MUIRON, CARRÈRE, REVANCHE and INDEPENDANT nearer to the land and home. When one of us became impatient to start the engine we would remind him that it must have been far more tantalising for the four ships, sixty-eight days out from Egypt and an agony of frustration for their principal and impetuous passenger.

But if the absence of wind persisted we would be persuaded by the argument that Napoleon would certainly have instructed Rear-Admiral Ganteaume to switch on the BMC Navigator if the flagship had possessed one. We would surrender and motor in.

It would take some powerful imagining in the gulf now to dream one's way back into the past for there are one, two, three large marinas within view and enough yachting traffic to require wide awake attention.

No other coast that I know has changed in recent years more than the French Mediterranean. New yacht harbours have appeared, little harbours have become big harbours, pontoons have sprouted everywhere, all in the last five—ten years? It all seems to have happened so quickly, before one's very eyes as it were. And all this quite apart from the ambitious new development in the Languedoc-Roussillon.

As new harbours are created so yachts are in them, just as though they had been built in with the harbours; you cannot help wondering where all these boats come from in their hundreds and thousands, also you cannot help wondering where they all go when they set off for a cruise. (This problem arises everywhere, of course. It only needs a small proportion of Solent-based yachts to sail to other Solent ports and you have congestion everywhere and empty berths somewhere else. Already temporary berth exchanges are being arranged in advance by telephone. Soon we shall need a computer to slot us all in; and then we shall not announce a proposed cruise to Lymington but a cruise on Computer D.F.)

They come to the French Mediterranean, of course, because it is the dream of every boat owner to sail or to keep his boat on this coast. It was always mine, I know; a vision of palm trees, brightly coloured pavement cafes just across the cobblestones from my clean alongside berth, blue translucent water, an orchestra playing, a bottle of Côtes du Provence on the cockpit table, warm sunshine, pleasant company, few clothes.

The cobble-stones have given way to smooth marina quays with instant mooring facilities besides water and electricity laid on; the quayside cafes and the palm trees are a few pontoons away; music, not always to your taste, is available from transistors as it is in marinas everywhere. The translucent water, the sun, the wine, a wider choice of company continue in apparently permanent and unlimited quantity.

Marina Style

Practically every port on the French Mediterranean coast is now 'marina style', but it would be naive to imagine that all the new gleaming harbours have been constructed for itinerant cruising folk like you and me. Developers have built the harbours to promote the sale of the surrounding apartments and villas that go with the reserved yacht parking places (or vice versa, perhaps); not exclusively so, of course, because so many public mooring places have been made available in even the most private development. And sometimes the French Government may approve only the harbour development and not that of the surrounding buildings, in which case the marina harbour must pay its way exactly like (but not always so expensive as) our marinas in England.

Building or planned are Port de Cannes Marina, a huge apartment-harbour complex on the Baie de La Napoule, six kilometres from Cannes at the mouth of the River Siagne; also an apartment plus hotel plan with some moorings on the Pointe de la Croisette; Port de Fontvieille, Monaco and Port de Cap d'Ail; by Nice Airport at Saint Laurent du Var; at Saint-Aygulf; Bormes-Les-Mimosas at Cap Bénat, Le Lavandou and Port de l'Ile de Bendor.

Obviously there are fewer construction problems when you can

The Yachtsman's Mecca

build solid concrete pontoons without tidal problems.

Demand hastens building activity everywhere except, possibly, in some of the remoter Languedoc-Roussillon harbours where developers wait for property sales to leapfrog over stage developments before proceeding. And there is no doubt whatever that the chief beneficiary from all this activity is the cruising yachtsman.

Nowhere else can the cruising man find such a selection, such a variety of harbours, such superior marinas. This coast is the yachtsman's Mecca indeed.

It is easy to imagine that so many new marina developments might have changed the character of those parts of France where they are situated; but it is not so. Antibes is Antibes, Bandol is Bandol, Cannes is Cannes, exactly as delightful as always but now equipped, one might say, with new 'marine front doors'. The exceptions are the new creations in the Languedoc-Roussillon, Port la Galère, Port de Marina Baie des Anges etc., where there was nothing there before.

To get to the Mediterranean most yachts from England come down through France rather than 'round the corner';—across the Bay of Biscay and past Gibraltar.

The difficulty is to decide which harbours to visit, and a very pleasant difficulty it is. Where you decide to visit will determine where you 'come out' into the Mediterranean. If you want to see, say, Bandol, St. Tropez and Corsica you will emerge either down the Rhône or from the St. Louis canal. If you want to visit the Languedoc-Roussillon coast you may emerge at Sète.

Cruise Planning

It is suggested that you read through the following summaries of the harbours

(1) West of the Rhône
(2) East of the Rhône
(3) of Corsica

spacing out a cruise that will take you to the places that you want to see. Then you can look up the detail pages of these harbours, arranged in geographic sequence in the same (1), (2), (3) groupings shown above, in the second half of the book.

Having decided the area of the French Mediterranean coast that you would first like to explore, you then need to determine the most convenient exit point from the inland waterways of France.

The summary starting on the next page may therefore be of help.

French Mediterranean Harbours

Waterway Routes out of France into the Mediterranean

1. *The Rhône.* Straight down the Rhône to the sea if your draft will cause you no anxiety at the river mouth. Commercial vessels take Route (2) below. In any case the Rhône exit into the Mediterranean is the least interesting route and the most trying to the navigator, because everything looks the same at the mouth of the Rhône and there are so few marks to identify. The pilot will leave you at Arles to cruise the last thirty miles. You must have Admiralty Chart 1805 and should examine most carefully the depths at the mouth before deciding to go this way. If you have to step your mast it is not convenient to do this at Arles.

2. *From Port St. Louis-du-Rhône into the Golfe de Fos.*
Twenty-six miles down the Rhône from Arles turn in 140° to port, through the lock and bridge into the basin of Port St. Louis. To starboard you will see the St. Louis Canal, a straight run into the Golfe de Fos.

3. *The canal route from Arles to Port de Bouc* is closed at the time of writing by the construction of the new lock approach at the Arles end. At the other end the canal will emerge in the vast new industrial region at Fos.

4. *From Le Grau-du-Roi* which is at the seaward end, past the swing bridge, of the canal from Aigues-Mortes. To get to Aigues-Mortes you cruise along the Beaucaire-Sète canal from Beaucaire, having turned out of the Rhône at Beaucaire. You must instruct your pilot not to take you as far as Arles.
You could also reach Aigues-Mortes from the Canal du Midi direction.

5. *From Sète*
(a) as in (4) above, out of the Rhône at Beaucaire but continue on the Beaucaire-Sète canal past Aigues-Mortes to Sète.
(b) from the Canal du Midi (coming from Bordeaux), across the Etang du Thau to Sète.

The Yachtsman's Mecca

6. *From Port la Nouvelle*
   (a) as in (4) above, out of the Rhône at Beaucaire but continue on the Beaucaire-Sète canal, behind Sète, into the Etang du Thau; across the etang into the Canal du Midi, turn down into the River Aude and the Canal de la Robine to la Nouvelle.
   (b) from the Canal du Midi (coming from Bordeaux), in to the Aude as above.

These routes are described in my book 'THROUGH THE FRENCH CANALS' (Nautical Publishing Company Limited).

French harbours west of the Rhône are all in the Languedoc-Roussillon development; they are 'State' harbours with the exception of CANET which is privately operated. Planning of this gigantic enterprise began in 1963; following two years of research the State bought thousands of acres of land, eliminated the mosquitoes which infested the vast marshy areas, planted trees, built roads, laid on water, electricity and telephones and excavated the new harbours. Having initiated the dream the French Government appointed Local Development Boards to create their own areas in the most imaginative way.

It is planned that all construction work will be completed by 'about 1975' and this part of the new project (and particularly the harbours that principally concern us), is clearly within the control of the planners. The development of the surrounding buildings, shops, apartments—the bringing to life of the whole project is clearly in the hands of prospective purchasers.

Looking at this vast enterprise from the sea it makes one think that the whole world must buy a piece of something here to make it pay.

It is certainly a brave and ambitious project and the harbours that have been built are splendid harbours, many offering lagoon sailing as well as sea sailing, for a network of lagoons and canals fringe the coast. But imagine creating villages from nothing, from countryside that is flat, unattractive, dusty and often windy to start with. Some of the new areas around the harbours are slowly coming to life (La Grande Motte is a lively oasis indeed), as pioneer spirits see investment opportunities in the building development, mostly adventures in architecture; old style shapes in bold new colours and materials, alleyways, courtyards, jumbles of levels and lines all bright and sparkling yet somehow sad against the surrounding desolation.

16   French Mediterranean Harbours

Harbours WEST of the Rhône—(LANGUEDOC-ROUSSILLON)

The land you see, all sand dunes and scrub fringing the etangs, is the edge of the Camargue. Giving Pointe de Beauduc a wide berth you set a course for Point de l'Espiguette. If you see a large church, apparently amidst the sand dunes, this is Stes. Maries-de-la-Mer. Gypsies from all over the world assemble here in May each year (but not 'water gypsies' for there is no harbour).

The first harbour is Port Camargue, a splendid new Languedoc-Roussillon construction and linked in the development scheme with Le Grau du Roi. The latter is an old town on the banks of the canal leading to Aigues-Mortes, mentioned above as a possible 'entry' to the Mediterranean. When visibility is good you can see the towers of Aigues-Mortes, like a fairytale castle, shimmering in the distance. Port Camargue is all new and there is nothing ashore.

Le Grau du Roi is not a very convenient point of call because the fishing boats occupy both banks up to the swing bridge. Watch for the current at the entrance if you do go in here.

Within view ahead is the striking new architecture of La Grande Motte, rising triumphantly out of what was a flat waste of scrub and sand. You must put in here to see this showpiece of the Languedoc-Roussillon. There are always British boats in here.

From this (above) . . .
    . . . to this (right) is Languedoc-Roussillon.

The Yachtsman's Mecca

West of the Rhône

After La Grande Motte a narrow strip of coast separates the sea from the etangs, a strip hardly wide enough to accommodate the cars and lorries moving as though on water when seen through the haze. You may be surprised to see barges moving apparently amongst the road traffic for the Beaucaire-Sète canal is in this coastal strip.

Carnon is the next port, with good harbour facilities and a little of old and new ashore. It is preferred to Palavas with which it is linked in the Languedoc-Roussillon scheme. The River Lez flows out to sea at Palavas, having crossed the Beaucaire-Sète canal, but only very small craft can make use of the river up to the crossing. The main value of Palavas to the yachtsman is its prominent water tower which acts as a splendid mark. You can also see the big town of Montpellier in the distance on a clear day.

The coastal strip, flat and sandy, continues to Sète, a few hours sailing away. This is a most interesting port, more water than land it seems and sometimes likened to a miniature Venice. From a Mediterranean shipping point of view it ranks second to

Sète—the popular 'exit' port.

French Mediterranean Harbours

West of the Rhône

Marseille but the shipping quays and yacht harbour are quite separate. Sète is probably the most popular exit port from the inland waterways of France because there are so many more facilities here than at any other exit port.

From Sète along to Cap d'Agde the narrow strip continues, separating the sea from the Etang du Thau. You can of course go in (at Sète), and sail around this etang if you are so inclined. It is about ten miles long and two miles wide with quite a lot of industry on its banks. The large groups of fishing boats that you encounter in the etang sometimes pose a 'which side to pass' problem. From the sea you obtain views of Marseillan which is probably the best yacht harbour in the etang, though a trifle scruffy ashore.

It is quite a long run in to the new marina of Cap d'Agde where there is some development ashore, all new and bright.

The coastal scenery improves and the mountainous background comes more into prominence as you approach the mouth of the River Hérault. The town of Agde is about two miles up the river which goes on to provide a small craft entry to the Canal du Midi. At the entrance to the Hèrault is la Tamarissiére.

Sand dunes dominate the coastal scene as you cruise along to Valras at the mouth of the River Orb. You will see the masts of yachts moored in the marina where there are all facilities but nothing of interest in the immediate vicinity of the harbour.

Sandy beaches extend beyond the estuary of the River Aude; through the glasses you can see the colourful crowds of the new holiday areas, particularly Narbonne-Plage, beyond which is Gruissan, a small fishing village in process of development as a new marina harbour for 1,500 boats.

The entrance to the Grau de la Vielle Nouvelle provides a break in the sandy coastline. Through this entrance you can see the Etang de l'Ayrolle, behind which craft may be observed moving along the Canal de la Robine mentioned earlier as a route from the inland waterways to the sea at La Nouvelle.

The jetties marking the entrance to Port la Nouvelle come a little way out into the sea to greet you. If you propose going in here you should keep a look-out for ships as the channel is not wide. There are all facilities at Port la Nouvelle but the attractions ashore are not inspiring.

Until recent years we used to sail from Port la Nouvelle to the next harbour of Port Vendres, only hours away. Now there is a selection of new development marinas in between.

The Yachtsman's Mecca

West of the Rhône

The coast is sandy with a background of snow-capped mountains. The first resort of Leucate-Barcarès is being laid out on the isthmus between the sea and the Etang de Salses. The harbour of Port Leucate is vast already with facilities for 1,800 boats. Unfortunately it is set in an area that at present resembles a desert. This is undoubtedly the sort of place in which to buy an apartment now, whilst properties are cheap to encourage development. The moorings and harbour facilities are first class.

Port Barcarès—Grau St. Ange can accommodate 250 boats. Looking towards the shore, through the haze and poor visibility that is a feature of this area, you may be surprised to see a 30,000-ton liner nearer in to the shore than you are. Do not be tempted to sail in on the theory that if there is enough water for a liner there is enough for you. This particular ship, the 'Lydia', is beached deliberately on the sands of Barcarès to provide a tourist centre of restaurants and night-life onboard. Fully lit at night it is to be hoped that she will not prove to be a 'Circe' of the Languedoc-Roussillon coast.

Between Leucate and Bacares, the beached liner 'Lydia' provides a tourist centre.

West of the Rhône

A short sail away is Canet, with the harbour in a newer state of construction than the nearby town which is quite charming. The splendid town of Perpignan is only a short distance away.

St. Cyprien, the next marina harbour for 1,000 boats, is more isolated but there are splendid facilities afloat and a selection of shops ashore.

Plans for Argelès have been approved and development is under way; the coast improves in scenic character as you approach Collioure, a Mediterranean dream harbour indeed but very small and the greater convenience of nearby Port Vendres may be preferred.

Rounding Cap Bear the red hills of the Côte Vermeille provide a colourful background to Banyuls, a charming little harbour for 300 boats and a well established winter resort.

The small anchorage of Cerbere is the last of the 'to be developed' ports of the Languedoc-Roussillon. Four kilometres beyond is Spain and a guide to the Spanish coastline is provided in my book, 'DOWN THE SPANISH COAST' (Nautical Publishing Company Limited).

To summarise the progress in the twenty harbours of what is to be the largest yachting centre in Europe:

1. LE GRAU DU ROI—PORT CAMARGUE—Although linked by name the former is an old town, the latter is all new.
2. LA GRANDE MOTTE—all new.
3. CARNON—Coastal strip joins with Palavas.
4. PALAVAS—New moorings above bridge.
5. SETE—To be developed.
6. SETE—existing.
7. CAP D'AGDE—New harbours and towns around them, but nearby is existing Agde and La Tamarissière.
8. VALRAS—to be developed.
9. EMBOUCHURE DE L'AUDE—To be developed.
10. GRUISSAN—To be developed.
11. PORT LA NOUVELLE—To be developed.
12. PORT LEUCATE—All new.
13. PORT BARCARES—GRAU ST. ANGE—All new.
14. PORT DE CANET—New harbour attached to existing Canet-Plage.
15. ST. CYPRIEN—All new.
16. ARGELES—To be developed.
17. COLLIOURE—To be developed.

The Yachtsman's Mecca

West of the Rhône
18. PORT VENDRES.
19. BANYULS—To be developed.
20. CERBERE—To be developed.

The Languedoc-Roussillon scheme covers approximately 110 miles of coast and aims to provide moorings for 15,000 boats and room for a similar number ashore.

It will be 'the biggest leisure area in the world'.

Harbours EAST of the Rhône—(THE COTE D'AZUR)

From the Rhône, round the shores of the Golfe de Fos and across to Marseille is a large area of industrial development in which Port de Bouc is the largest harbour. If you have come straight down the Rhône there is no point in going back up into the Golfe de Fos to visit Port Bouc as it is not sufficiently attractive to merit such a diversion. But if you have come from the Rhône through the St. Louis canal, Port Bouc will be almost on the way.

If you wished to visit the intriguing fishing port of Martigues you would go in here at Port Bouc, along the Canal de Caronte into the Etang de Berre but there is industry all around and urgent shipping serving it. In bad weather you get surprisingly large waves in the gulf.

Between here and Marseille you will see rocky headlands, small coves, factory chimneys in an otherwise bare coastline and there are only small harbours that are not suitable for the average cruising yacht. Carro, for instance, which should be given a wide

Carro.

French Mediterranean Harbours

East of the Rhône

berth as you prepare to round Cap Couronne for you can see the rocks extending offshore. Port de Sausset is mainly a fishing boat harbour and Port de Carry is difficult to enter without local knowledge.

In any case Marseille is so near that no problem arises. A visit to Marseille is a must, an exciting nautical experience and you will leave it exhausted or exhilarated.

Some say that the Côte d'Azur stretches from Toulon to Nice, others from Marseille to Menton.

Leaving Marseille and passing the Château d'If, which recalls the Count of Monte Cristo, round the islands by Cap Croisette, it is no more than a five hour cruise to Cassis. Your chart will indicate the various islands, none of which is of particular interest. The only other shelter before Cassis is at Sormiou, protected from the S.W. but it can only be considered as an anchorage. You will see quite a lot of boats in the harbour but they are small.

The huge rock formations, the calanques of Cassis, provide an exciting picture and colour contrast.

Having rounded Cacao Point, turning in to the Bay of Cassis, you will see another display of masts at Port Miou but they belong to small boats only though a larger development is planned here; the larger and more attractive harbour of Cassis is visible ahead.

The coastline of red rocks carries on and La Ciotat is just round Cap de l'Aigle. If the sight of the huge shipbuilding cranes at La Ciotat puts you off do not despair, for the delightful

La Ciotat is a shipbuilding town set in a beautiful bay.

The Yachtsman's Mecca

East of the Rhône

harbour of Bandol is just around the next corner, with Sanary and the beautiful marina on the Iles des Embiez just beyond.

You can really relax now; this is what you have come for. Here are the palm trees, the sunshine, the pavement cafes; the interminable games of boule on the quay at Bandol.

Do not be in too much of a hurry to move on from these three, Bandol, Sanary and Embiez; you have equal beauty, considerable interest and considerable excitement ahead it is true but there is a tranquility about these harbours that you may not recapture again.

The harbour at Le Brusc, by the way, is too small and too crowded to be considered but extensions are planned.

From Cap Sicie you alter course to round Cap Cépet and so enter Toulon Bay. The splendid harbour of St. Mandrier is in to port, past the Naval Establishment. There is a good bus service from here up to Toulon and a bus ride to view the yacht harbour there may persuade you that it is less peaceful than St. Mandrier. You will pass La Seyne, a nice little harbour if it was set in other surroundings but it happens to be in the middle of dockyard industry.

There is no harbour in the Gulf of Giens. A few hours sail will bring you between the end of the Giens Peninsula and the Ile de Porquerolles. You sometimes get quite a choppy sea coming through here, it arrives suddenly so hang on to your bottle of blanc de blanc if it happens to be in an exposed position. Port du Niel, at the end of the peninsula, is too small to merit our consideration which is a pity for it is most attractive.

The choice now lies between turning to port in to the Hyeres Road and up to Hyeres or to the nearer Porquerolles Harbour to starboard. I would advise you to see Porquerolles because it is unusual; it has been likened to the Garden of Eden which may entrance you or bore you but it is certainly different.

Hyeres is a splendid harbour with an interesting town about two miles away. From Hyeres you can set a course to round Cap Blanc for there is no other adequate yachting harbour in this bay.

Or from Porquerolles you may be interested to see the other islands. Ile de Port-Cros is rugged and not so easy of access as Porquerolles as there is less than 1 m depth on the small jetties. The scenery on the Ile du Levant may be more to your liking for it happens to be a nudist colony, quite established and provider of postcard subjects for many resorts for miles around. Recently one of the French Armed Services set up a base on the

East of the Rhône

island, no doubt enjoying a subsequent improvement in recruiting figures. It is possible to anchor off and land by dinghy on the Ile du Levant.

As you sail back to the mainland coast, along towards Cavalaire, it is interesting to reflect that this was the coast chosen for the landing of American and French forces thirty years ago (in August 1944).

Le Lavandou is a splendid little marina harbour, clean, surrounded by a smooth outline of mountains and nearer, the rich green of the hills, with nearer still the brilliant colours of the flowers around the harbour. If this was the only harbour it would send you wild with delight, but you have already seen so many, and you have so many more to see, so by comparison, Le Lavandou is quite ordinary.

It is only a short sail from Le Lavandou to Cavalaire but the harbour and surroundings here are quite uninspiring. It might be preferred to set a course to clear Cap Lardier and make for the selection of more exciting harbours around the corner in the Gulf of St. Tropez, either St. Tropez, les Marines de Cogolin, Port Grimaud or Ste. Maxime.

The Pilot warns of an area in the Golfe de St. Tropez in which aircraft carry out various weapon practices and you should make a point of looking for this on your chart.

St. Tropez you will no doubt approach with the greatest anticipation in view of its reputation, but be prepared to be disappointed; you will be in the outer harbour and the glamour quay inside will be jammed with the huge yachts of millionaire industrialists. The harbours further in to the bay reflect the same aura of sophistication and my main interest here, you may be surprised to learn, is connected with pipe smoking.

The dark green wooded mountains that have been providing your background to the coastal strip since Hyeres are the Maures Mountains. If you are a pipe smoker you may be interested to learn that some of the best pipes in the world come from here. I always try to get up to Cogolin to add a few more to my collection; really beautiful and satisfyingly smokable pipes are displayed in large numbers and cost a quarter of the price of pipes in England.

Ste. Maxime is a fashionable resort with a splendid harbour, while the two ports of St. Raphael are a short sail away, offering such perfect sailing if the weather is kind as it usually is, with a background of red rocks contrasting with the blue sea.

East of the Rhône

The harbour of St. Aygulf is too small to be of interest and, anyhow, St. Raphael appears too soon as it is. The old harbour is up at the head of the bay, the new marina is across on the Pointe des Lions.

St. Raphael marks the beginning of the Esterel Coast with its red rocks, green vegetation and the blue sea skipping in and out amongst the bays and creeks. Agay is only a small harbour, no more than an anchorage and exposed to the S.E.

Le Trayas is a new harbour. Although attractive it is not of much interest to the cruising yacht unless you happen to carry a car on your foredeck like the barges. There are no shops within miles but there is a restaurant actually on the quay.

The beautiful creeks and bays, the contrasting colours of rocks and vegetation, sandy coves washed by the bluest sea, the beauty and continuing beauty of this coast it is easy to take for granted after a time. It is difficult to single out a particular part of the coastline as being beautiful because it all is.

Port la Galere, described as a marine paradise, consists of new apartment buildings blended on to a magnificent rocky promontory. At the foot is the harbour which happens to have a rather difficult approach but, once in, it is pleasant and there is a shop on the quay. Apart from this there is nothing of interest ashore except the striking architecture of Port la Galere itself.

The harbours on this part of the coast are so near to each other; leaving Port la Galere you scarcely have time to hoist a sail before you are round the Point de l'Aiguille and abreast of the small harbour of Theoule. Port de la Rague is there, just beyond Theoule, and Port de Mandelieu—La Napoule just beyond that.

Theoule is the old harbour, very small, up in the corner of the Golfe de la Napoule. It has the advantage of being in the town so that there is interest ashore, but one is tempted by the greater yachting attractions of the newer and glossier Port de la Rague within view. The yacht facilities here are new and splendid with good chandlers' shops in the port area, but outside of it is just a road.

The same road is outside the next habour of Port de Mandelieu—La Napoule, an enormous area of quays with room for 1,500 boats; but at least there is a good selection of shops on the quay here including a laundrette.

And so you come to Cannes, surely the most fabulous yachting port in the world. In the harbour and ashore there is everything

East of the Rhône

that money can buy and of course it gets crowded. But like rich food, you can only take so much and you steal away after a time in search of peace.

Port Pierre-Canto, at the other end of the bay, is quite an impressive harbour but in the middle of a residential district.

Peace may be found at the Iles de Lerins comprised of Ile St. Honorat and Ile Ste. Marguerite, beautiful islands of pine forests. There is a Cistercian Monastery on St. Honorat and you can anchor off, watching your anchor and chain all the way down in the crystal clear water, and row ashore to the tiny harbour.

A cell in the fort on Ile St. Marguerite is famous as the prison of the Man in the Iron Mask (imprisoned for eleven years, 1687–98, by Louis XIV; died 1703 in the Bastille).

Round the Point de la Croisette you have a view ashore of leisure and pleasure traffic, so you realise that the full beauty of the coastline could never be fully appreciated from the land; the soft green hills with a ribbon of sand just separating them from the blue sea, the white and pink washed buildings embraced by pines, the riotous colour of a thousand beach umbrellas against the pink of the buildings. Not only do you have a superior vantage point of this glorious technicolour scene but it is silent. The inferior vantage points ashore are very much in sound.

Golfe Juan is a short sail away. The harbour here is small but pleasant and with the advantage of being in the town.

Although on opposite sides of Cap d'Antibes, Juan les Pins and Antibes have joined into a single holiday resort. At fashionable Juan there is no harbour but just along the coast is Port Gallice, said to be at Antibes which, from a yachting point of view is round the corner and fifteen kilometres away. A private harbour in residential surroundings, Port Gallice is not of much interest to the cruising yachtsman.

Port Vauban, in Antibes, is of much greater interest because you have all facilities in great profusion and shoreside interest all around.

From here the coastal focal point is the road, in fact two roads and you can watch the jangle of traffic round the edge of the Baie des Anges from the calm peace of your cockpit.

You will not be in any doubt as to its identity when you sight Port Marina Baie-des-Anges. The huge apartment blocks climb up into the sky like swaying switchbacks. The harbour is pleasant and modern and there are shops in the port area. Outside is the main road only.

The Yachtsman's Mecca

The distinctive architecture of Baie des Anges.

The nearby harbour of Cros-de-Cagnes is suitable for small boats only.

Your privileged position of sea-going peace is shattered as you cruise towards Nice. Big jet planes from Nice Airport struggle up into the sky leaning over you, ease down slowly on black smoke trails, shattering your senses with sound. Nice is set in a sounding drum of hills, the noise goes beyond noise and becomes a sensation. But you forgive Nice, the beautiful, because she has always offered everything except peace. Anyone who has staggered back to his yacht during the reign of King Carnival at Nice would not go back there for a rest cure.

The yacht harbour is at the far end of the bay, right in the old town with traffic careering on three sides. A stroll across the road to fetch your *Daily Telegraph* from the shop on the corner is dicing with death. I like peace and I like Nice; it is the effect it has on you.

But just around the Cap de Nice is the tranquil Bay of Villefranche with the harbour right up in the bay to port. Villefranche has a special appeal because it never seems to change.

Cruising along the coast of Cap Ferrat you marvel at the houses of the wealthy; tucked away round the corner is the beautiful little harbour of St. Jean-Cap-Ferrat. It has changed in

French Mediterranean Harbours

East of the Rhône

recent years, enlarged to twice its former size and yet retains its charm.

And then Beaulieu, within view, a dream yacht harbour of flowers and palm trees; then Monaco . . . where else in the world is the yachtsman offered such riches within so small an area of coastline? And where else, unfortunately, are so many yachts seeking such riches? At the height of the season France is impossibly crowded everywhere, afloat and ashore, but early and late you will get in and, of course, the mooring tariffs are all substantially cheaper from October to May.

We came across a picture of myself, sitting in the cockpit eating Christmas pudding, dressed in shorts only on the 25th December at Nice. But, of course, this is the warm end of the coast and you would never sit in any open cockpit in Marseille during December unless you had a fur coat on.

May is the best time. In the soft still of the mornings, drifting just off this extravagantly beautiful coast you seem to feel the fragrance off the land and are mesmerised by it until that other most acceptable fragrance comes wafting up into the cockpit . . . the smell of coffee.

As you approach Monaco the construction work that you see is the new development of Port de Fontvieille. The unmistakable Port de Monaco is just beyond.

A few miles further on this fabulous coastline, round Cap Martin, and the Côte d'Azur comes to an end at Menton. The less attractive Port Communal is in the old part and the new Port Garavan is in the residential part. You will, I think, prefer Port Garavan as we do, but the town is charming and enjoys the mildest climate on the Riviera.

Five minutes away is Italy.

Five minutes past Port Garaven is Italy.

The Yachtsman's Mecca

Corsica

'A mountain surrounded by sea', says the brochure. To get to it the plane takes forty minutes, the steamer seven hours, you and I about twenty hours. Perhaps because it is a night sail away from the Côte d'Azur marinas it will never be crowded.

Whether or not your fix is on the nose your first view of Corsica is one of wonderment. It is accepted that the best view of Corsica is the view from the sea. You survey steep tall mountains, folds of tree-covered rich green mountains, jagged brown bare mountains, snow covered giants of mountains with white clouds resting on their shoulders.

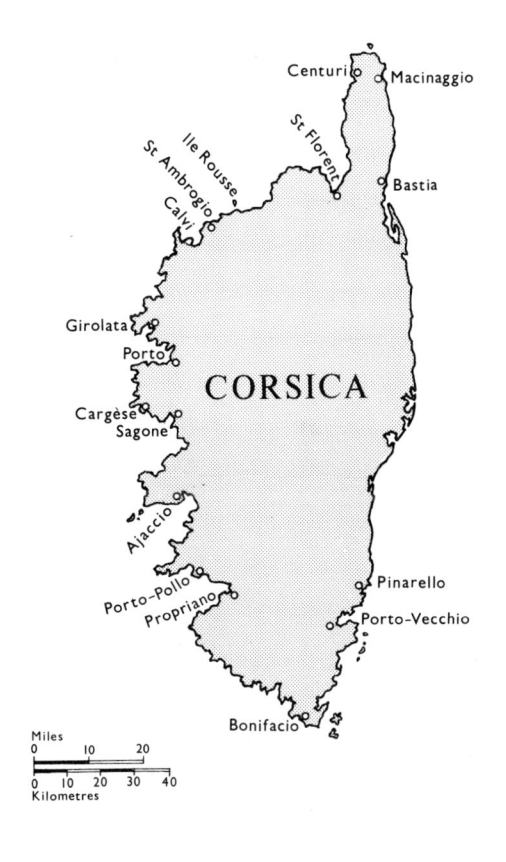

Corsica

A road runs along much of the coastline. Standing off you see the glint of the sun on the windscreens of cars that appear to be clinging like flies to green precipices; through the glasses you pick out a distinctive vehicle and watch it, now high up, now low down, now facing one way, now another.

Taking a bearing, say on the de la Pietra light, the white square building and tower perched on the brown rock all seem to emanate waves of the heat that is blistering you in the cockpit; and yet beyond and above, in line, you see snow.

Valleys and deep ravines come down to the sea in welcoming bays with rich brown sands utterly deserted; the blue of the sea, the brown of the sand, the green of the grass, shrubs and trees make such a picture of unspoilt perfection that you feel you must abandon your programme and anchor just there, for ever perhaps. Then, round the headland is another perfect bay and another, until you realise that much of this coast of Corsica is such a paradise.

Adam and Eve had a nice spot too, we are taught, but they obviously had no problems with empty water tanks nor Camping Gaz refills. With such considerations in mind and, more important, the need to safeguard your vessel against wind and waves, you can only prudently consider visiting the perfect bays for limited stays and must seek the harbours for shelter and provisions.

Corsica is about the size of Wales, yet has a population of less than 300,000. The main towns on the west coast are Ajaccio and Calvi, on the east coast, Bastia. Bonifacio is at the bottom of the island facing Sardinia.

There is no marina development on the island in the sense that there is on the mainland coast, but improvements are taking place (if marina developments improve such a paradise). There is a private harbour plus apartments development at St. Ambrogio but it is on a small scale, also a larger development at Bonifacio and plans for Macinaggio.

The rocky west coast of Corsica is considered to be the most beautiful being heavily indented with bays and inlets, whereas the east coast, low and straight, is hardly indented at all although the northern part is more interesting. Since the bays and inlets are on the coast nearest to France it will be most convenient if a description of the Corsican coastline starts at Calvi, nearest harbour to France and, because of this, usually the first port of call.

The Yachtsman's Mecca

The rocky west coast of Corsica is heavily indented with bays and inlets.

It is quite a long way all round Corsica (the actual coastline roughly equals the length of the French Mediterranean coast), so the majority of cruising yachts sail down the west coast from Calvi to Bonifacio, in through the Bonifacio Strait, and then down the east coast of Sardinia.

It so happens that Calvi is a perfect yachting harbour, some consider it to be the best and most beautiful in Corsica, and its perfection is only spoilt because so many other yachtsmen share this view. At the height of the season it is too internationally smart for comfort but in May and early June it is pleasantly uncrowded as a rule.

From Calvi, coming down the west coast, the next stop might be the anchorage at Girolata—I was going to say 'isolated and beautiful' but this description applies with equal emphasis to every bay on this coast, more than are mentioned here. And isolated they are indeed for some are only accessible from the sea.

Porto is set amidst red cliffs and green valleys, Cargesse is an open anchorage by (another) beautiful sandy beach; the beautiful bays and beaches continue, there is always one in view so that you wonder if this is the beautiful bay you were looking at just

Corsica now or is it another one? For there are no buildings, beach umbrellas, or people to provide points of recollection; there is not even a footprint in the golden sand. It is difficult, amidst so much beauty, not to sound like a travel brochure.

At the beautiful bay of Sagone there is a small quay but nothing behind it except a little road leading away into the valleys and trees; there is no sign of life and if provisions were needed it would be more convenient to carry on to Ajaccio.

Ajaccio is a big harbour, much bigger than Calvi, a town harbour in a setting of impressive mountains. There are all facilities here and the town is a charming place to wander in, with statues at every turn to remind you whose birthplace this is.

Continuing down the coast, round the Pte. Guardiola, you come to Porto Pollo—an anchorage with some life ashore in the shape of a hamlet and some past life in the shape of neolithic caves a little way inland.

Propriano is a port on the visiting list of steamers and is pleasant enough though small. The mole running out parallel to the quay gives protection from westerly winds but it can be uncomfortable here with the wind in the north.

You often see yachts anchored in the river inlet of Figari but the confidence of local knowledge is required to go right in here for you see rocks everywhere.

And so you come to the bottom of the island at Bonifacio which has as dramatic an entrance as any harbour in the world as you cruise in between skyscraper cliff sides.

Continuing up the east coast the first harbour of interest is Porto-Vecchio, over two miles up at the head of the gulf of the same name. Nelson considered this to be the best anchorage in the island, though somewhat unhealthy. From some points of view it does not seem to have altered much since Nelson's day except that there are now some modern facilities available.

Pinarello is not very inspiring and the next harbour of any note is over a hundred kilometres away at Bastia. Here the background to the bustling yacht harbour looks like a stage set with tall 17th century buildings looking right down on you, almost as though you were moored in the orchestra stalls.

The peninsula of Cap Corse is about fifty kilometres long with many beautiful bays and inlets. Near the top (still on the eastern side), is Macinaggio but it is rather small for the average cruising yacht.

Rounding the top of Cap Corse, the Cap Corse road, you see

The Yachtsman's Mecca

The cliffs seen from the town of Bonifacio at the bottom of the island.

Giraglia island but nothing of interest is there.

Returning down the western side the first harbour is at Centuri where you turn in before the island. It is mainly a fishing boat harbour and very small.

Saint-Florent is a new harbour that has been built for the yachtsman. Needless to say it is in a beautiful setting and there are shops and shore attractions within view of your berth; in fact Saint-Florent is a splendid alternative to Calvi as your arrival port in Corsica. It is certainly less crowded and has a larger and more modern quay area for yachts.

Ile-Rousse, too, is another 'first stop' alternative although the facilities, at the time of writing, are not so convenient as at Saint-Florent. But the yachting potential at Ile-Rousse is being developed and the town, although a good walk away, is larger than Saint-Florent and most attractive. The Ile-Rousse that you visit is not, in fact, an island. There are adjacent islands in

Corsica what is known as the Ile-Rousse group.
From Ile-Rousse it is a short sail back to Calvi.

The best seasons in which to visit Corsica are from mid-May when the maquis is in flower (thus 'the scented isle'), through June and from September to mid-October.

There is no doubt that the best view of Corsica is the view from the sea.

2 Suitable and Unsuitable Boats

A chapter on these lines has been included in my previous books. In writing it I am influenced by the letters I have received and the questions I have been asked by prospective long distance cruising folk. The majority of these are novices and I must therefore ask the knowledgeable yachtsman to bear with me if some of the points raised appear to be elementary.

It is argued that people without experience should not put to sea but they do, in increasing numbers, and will, unless legislation is introduced to prevent them.

Novices are in the majority of those who set off on long distance cruises through France to the Mediterranean but I have concluded that their ambition and determination to go is an indication of their fitness to succeed. Seamanship relies largely on common sense and good manners as anyone who sails in the Solent will sadly observe.

We have lost count of the number of times that novice cruising folk in Le Havre have asked if they can follow us across to the entrance to the Seine. It seems that beginners on a big adventure are not afraid to ask and this is their strength. The week-end novice continues to come alongside with the tide because he knows it all and appears to resent advice.

Beginners start asking when they are seeking a boat. I suspect that they seek my opinion in the hope that it will agree with the one they have already formed; but if not, they appreciate some mental digestion before swallowing their conviction.

You may judge the extent of my influence when I mention a gentleman in South Africa who wrote that he was giving up his business there to take a boat through the French Canals, having read my book on the subject. For this I advise almost any craft

French Mediterranean Harbours

of suitable draft EXCEPT multi-hulls. Some time later we came into Le Havre after dark and tied up to what appeared to be a pontoon secured alongside the pontoon. Morning revealed it to be a catamaran and (you have guessed), in command was the gentleman from South Africa.

In my last book I mentioned displacement motor cruisers in particular reference to the extended living aboard, say three to six months, desirable for a Mediterranean cruise. I have since received letters pointing out that I did not mention the motion at sea of this type of craft.

Some cruisers roll more than others of course. Displacement hulls roll more than planing hulls, all motor craft roll more than all sailing craft under sail on most points of the wind. Part of the answer with a motor cruiser is to have a steadying sail and another part of the answer is not to go out if the sea is rough.

Displacement motor cruiser with a steadying sail.

A glance at the distances between ports on the French Mediterranean coast will show that you are never far from a harbour. And you see so many displacement motor cruisers in the Mediterranean that they must have many points in their favour for cruising the sea of seas. The bigger ones are fitted with mini-stabilisers of course.

Suitable and Unsuitable Boats

Most boats are bought without any suggestion of a trial run. Many new owners and their wives (particularly their wives), have been sick with dismay, in addition to mal-de-mer, on discovering that their new boat, steady as a rock at the Boat Show, actually rolls about at sea.

Unless the motion is extremely bad I do assure you that you get used to it, in fact you forget all about it until you have a visitor on board who complains. In no time at all you step ashore to notice the quay moving under your feet instead and you are then a sea dog indeed.

But do have a trial run before you buy your boat.

Although every displacement motor cruiser has a characteristic motion all its own, do not let these remarks deter you from buying one. The sea is not always rough and, in any case, you spend far more time at moorings than you do at sea. For your voyage to the Mediterranean you will have three weeks or so cruising down through France when the only motion you will experience will be from the wash of passing craft. If you are turning west when you reach the Mediterranean you can go along the Beaucaire-Sète canal to reach the sea and then there will always be a French harbour within three hours cruising. If you turn eastwards from the Rhône you have no more than five hour trips initially and then no harbour is more than a few hours cruise away. The crossing to Corsica takes us about twenty-two hours under sail and approximately fourteen hours under power, Nice to Calvi being about the same distance as from Southampton to Le Havre.

Another reason for having a trial run is to determine the amount of engine noise. You must have diesel power, for a petrol motor is impossibly expensive. Some diesel engines, particularly the smaller ones, are about as quiet as a pneumatic drill, intolerable to cruise with for long periods. Because a boat and engine is new does not mean at all that the engine will be quiet. We were invited to make the short trip across from Hyeres to Porquerolles in a gleaming new 35-footer with twin Z-drives and you can judge the effect on my ear drums when I tell you that I did not even hear the proud owner inviting me to open a bottle of Château Simone.

Have the largest amount of living accommodation that you can afford, but the answer for the majority is a boat not so large that you need a crew. Everybody wants a bigger boat inside than it is outside; no boat will ever be perfect and every choice is a compromise. You search for years to find a suitable craft and when you get it the first thing you do is to alter it. People with money spend much time and thought in planning their perfect specification. When completed they tell you, 'In my next boat I shall have it this way,' and so on and so on.

For a long cruise you must have comfort, and the displacement motor cruiser has been mentioned as providing the most comfort per given L.O.A. It is also the easiest type of boat to handle and the BEECHAM illustrated is a good example, every inch of room having been designed for comfortable living and with the power units tucked away under the wheel-house.

Beecham 45.

You will note from the illustration that an outside steering position has been fitted and this is a very desirable feature, not only to enjoy the sunshine and the view but for ease of manoeuvring when coming into harbour. The outside steering position should not be so high out of the water as to preclude a voyage down through France. (The heights of fixed bridges in the inland waterways are given in my book *Through The French Canals.*)

The dinghy in stern davits, on the other hand, is not a desirable feature for the journey down through the inland waterways and it would then be stowed on deck. Once in the Mediterranean a dinghy is rarely used for coming ashore on the French coast because you invariably secure alongside so the use of the dinghy does not arise until you get to Corsica.

Suitable and Unsuitable Boats

An aft cabin for permanent sleeping quarters is almost a necessity when you are living onboard for long periods. To have to live and sleep in the same cabin, rolling up beds before you can have your breakfast, gets very tiresome after a week or so. Aft cabins can be found on motor cruisers with quite a modest waterline length.

Aft cabins are available on sailing cruisers too, of course, and it would appear that more people want to *sail* from one French harbour to another than to *motor*. In this connection it is interesting to note that sailing craft are charged less than motor craft in some French Mediterranean harbours.

However strongly one asserts that sailing in the Mediterranean is a disappointment, nobody believes you until they try. But at least it is wise not to have too much sail with a crew of only two; another alternative is to have an easily managed sail plan such as a ketch.

The Seadog shown is an admirable example of an easily

Seadog.

Photo:
Eileen Ramsey.

French Mediterranean Harbours

handled rig, plus an aft cabin, plus a dinghy stowed inboard, adding up to a splendid type of sailing yacht for a Mediterranean cruise and for the inland waterway journey to get there.

There are many centre cockpit motor-sailers, most of them larger than the 30ft L.O.A. of the Seadog. It must be admitted, however, that there are no ketches in the secondhand market in the lower price range and many letters I receive from would be adventurers want an inexpensive but roomy sailing boat.

Best known of the aft cabin sloops is the Hillyard 9-tonner which could be bought second-hand for about half the price of the ketch mentioned above. You see these familiar double-enders in harbours all over the world.

Hillyard, 9 ton sloop.

Suitable and Unsuitable Boats

Cheaper again would be a second-hand Atalanta, built of hot moulded marine ply said to be impervious to marine borers. This craft also has the unique feature of retractable bilge keels, useful if you have the misfortune to go aground in the virtually non-tidal Mediterranean.

We have talked to all sorts of people in all sorts of boats in the Mediterranean and have yet to meet anyone who regretted their decision, although most have admitted to the most serious qualms before setting off. It is an adventure absolutely 'tailor made' for retired people because it provides a moderate amount of physical exertion in fresh air and sunshine and, most important, the most challenging antidote to the boredom that assails the retired. We

Atalanta 31.

have met hundreds of retired couples cruising in the Mediterranean, happier and healthier than they have ever been in their lives.

Most husband and wife crews easily manage a cruise down through France and along the French Mediterranean coast; some have help across to Le Havre but not all by any means. Once in the Mediterranean you do not have to struggle and strain when mooring. You come into a harbour, look around, stop, deliberate, light your pipe if you like, no tide is going to whisk you away. In most marina harbours you will be seen and directed; if not, you move slowly towards the Capitainerie often at, or near to, the harbour entrance (the position of each Capitainerie is shown on the detail pages). It helps if you are efficient at manoeuvring astern and you should certainly practice this.

We have also met many very junior yachtsmen (and yachtswomen), on the long distance cruising scene. You see craft dressed overall with nappies, playpens on deck, baby carriages on the quay, the parents (of all nationalities), having decided to get away for a year or so before their children anchored them to a non-boating existence.

Many of these people were not living and working in the sort of situation where a Mediterranean cruise seemed possible. But they decided to go . . . and went.

More important than the choice of boat is the making of the decision to go. Many people have been writing to me for years about the proposed trip they are making next year, always next year, when they have saved enough money for the boat they want.

In the Mediterranean harbours the rich and the poor boats rub strakes together, but it is the poor wot gets the pleasure and the rich wot gets the ulcers, to paraphrase, roughly, the popular song.

In St. Jean-Cap-Ferrat we were alongside a 21ft sloop, all that her bronzed young owners could afford. If they had waited to save for something better they would not have been sitting in the sunshine at Cap Ferrat . . . and they might not have gone at all.

Most long distance cruising folk agree that the biggest factor in the whole venture is the making of the decision to do it. After that everything clicks into shape.

3 Equipment

To get to the French Mediterranean coast you will probably cruise down through the French canals and the equipment needed for the inland waterway journey is set out in *Through The French Canals* (Nautical Publishing Company Limited).

Briefly these items are:

A dinghy that will stow inboard out of the way

At least four 15 fathom 1½ to 2in warps

Necessary flags

Adequate fenders; a minimum of four, sausage shape

Motor tyres, one for each 4ft of waterline; you will, of course, dispose of these on arrival in the Mediterranean

A plank for hanging outside of the tyres when alongside piles, also to double up as a gangplank

A ladder

Boathooks and a pole for fending off in descending, sloping sided locks

A searchlight

A hooter or syren

Torches

Planned-in-advance stowage on deck for masts, where applicable.

Stepping the Mast If you have a sailing boat the first task will be to step your mast. The most convenient 'exit' ports for this purpose are Port St. Louis, Sète or Port la Nouvelle; in the latter harbour there is a very convenient bridge over the waterway near the yacht moorings. You will need spare blocks to rig a tackle and these should be included amongst your equipment. Spare mast bolts, in fact spare any rigging items not actually attached to the mast should be taken. In the excitement and exertion of stepping a

French Mediterranean Harbours

Trailers mast it is surprising what goes over the side.
If you have a boat that can be towed on a trailer it is worth considering this quicker method of getting it to the Mediterranean if time is limited. Facilities exist, particularly in the Languedoc-Roussillon, for lifting in and out of the water.

You should allow yourself a day or so to step the mast and to restow gear, equipment and provisions. Be careful not to stow tins near to the compass which will now be brought into use again; it is easily done when store cupboards are sited on bulkheads the other side of which might be the compass only inches away. Take some test bearings before you set off on your Mediterranean cruise to satisfy yourself that all is well.

Your normal items of navigational gear will be normal for the Mediterranean too; nothing special is necessary except for the appropriate charts and sailing directions, *Mediterranean Pilot Vol II* (46).

The equipment needed for your boat is not so much specifically related to the requirements of a Mediterranean cruise as to the requirements of living onboard for the length of time that such a cruise entails. Obviously these requirements should all be attended to before you leave your home port.

Homely Touches You see items on many boats not connected with the business of cruising at all, for instance plants in flower pots and small flower beds in boxes, corner cupboards of purely decorative china and family portraits in silver frames, homely touches that many women need in order to accept that, for the time being at least, the boat is their home.

The boat is their home.

You cannot have too many lockers and cupboards. Any spare space should be utilised for fixing ready-made cupboards that you can buy at do-it-yourself shops or big stores.

Although extended living onboard calls for adequate water capacity, say one hundred gallons for two people, there are readily available supplies in all French Mediterranean harbours so that frequent topping up is no problem, and of course there are splendid showers in all marinas (not always free by any means). In Corsica there is not the same availability so that you would need to carry spare five-gallon containers for extra capacity and also for fetching supplies. If your water supply is electrically operated you should carry with you a spare pump as British spares and replacements abroad never seem to be exactly what you want. Find out how to effect repairs to your plumbing system. Even a small leak in an electrically operated water

Equipment 45

supply produces irritating grunts from the pump. Of course there is expert service available in most French harbours but labour is expensive.

Hosing Decks   Whilst on the subject of water you must make a practice of hosing down decks every day in the Mediterranean heat. And whilst on the subject of decks you must show the greatest respect for other people's decks if you have reason to go onboard. Some owners draw attention to this with a polite reminder at the gangway.

Cooking   The most important job of cooking is done by bottled gas which should be properly installed and tested. You should also make sure that every gas appliance onboard has adequate ventilation, for any fuel uses up fresh air. As an extra precaution you can fit a gas detector that sounds an alarm if gas is escaping. If you hear the alarm the first thing to do is to turn off all appliances and the gas at the cylinder; the next thing is to ventilate as briskly as possible.

You will probably know that Calor Gas is not obtainable abroad and you will need an adaptor (sold where Calor gas is sold), to convert the Camping Gaz that you buy in France to your system. The 6 lb containers of Camping Gaz cost about £1 and last two people for approximately ten days. They are available everywhere in France, not only in harbour areas.

Calor containers usually have their made-to-measure stowage onboard and the 6 lb Camping Gaz container will fit the stowage space of the small Calor bottle. If you have sufficient height at the stowage locker, or if you normally use the large Calor cylinders, you will find it much more economical to use the butane equivalent large sizes rather than Camping Gaz. Going down through France we usually change over at the fuel barges just the other side of Rouen but you see the big butane gas cylinders in most harbour areas in France.

When you change over cylinders you will obviously remember the pilot lights on your water heater and refrigerator.

Refrigerators   You must have a refrigerator for Mediterranean living. If you are buying one for the trip get the biggest you can instal; whatever size you buy will be too small. A bottled gas refrigerator needs the gas permanently on but safeguards provide that if the flame should be blown out the supply of gas would be automatically cut off.

Water Heaters   The same sort of device is fitted to the water heater. A water heater is not as necessary as a refrigerator in the Mediterranean, but it is very convenient to have hot water at the turn of the sink or washbasin tap.

Electric Power The electricity supply to your boat is not a problem on the French Mediterranean coast because the majority of marina berths have individual connections with all sorts of voltages, 12, 24, 110 and 220v but mostly 110v.

We still take the precaution of always carrying a generator onboard as well, believing the Basic Law of Batteries to be that they only run down in impossibly inconvenient situations.

Electric light is most convenient, easy and clean on a boat and the marina charges include a charge for the supply (the first free days in some harbours are never free of electricity). We have a sentimental attachment to our faithful Tilley lamp but he does rather warm up the cabin on hot Mediterranean nights.

Fans Another item of electrical equipment that you simply must have is a fan. You can buy small and efficient models at most chandlers. Finding the best position to fit them needs a lot of thought for not many boats have sufficient headroom to allow a fan to be fitted to the deckhead.

It is pleasant but not absolutely necessary to have deck awnings and the necessary frames and fittings to cover what is to be your sun deck. My wife always argues that if we take awnings we shall not need them, but I should mention that she is in charge of stowage and they do take up rather a lot of space in a small boat.

Fire Extinguishers You will not, I hope, need me to remind you of the necessity for fire extinguishers.

The quality of the water supply you can rely upon everywhere, but if you prefer the bottled variety you may be interested to learn that the new plastic bottles, with the bottoms cut off, make excellent funnels. The trouble about this sort of economy suggestion is that nothing gets thrown away.

And finally, an item of deck equipment that should come in for more moderate use in the Mediterranean is the boathook. If you have come down through the French canals you must forget your prowess as a foredeck jouster. You are going to be coming alongside expensive yachts who will not love you at all if they see you approaching with a nasty metal spike about to gouge their immaculate decks. Stern-to mooring is the general rule and there are various aids. At La Grande Motte there are lines from the quay to spacing/mooring posts ahead; some marinas have a bow mooring line running to a ring set in the quay astern which you

Equipment 47

Mooring aids . . . La Grande Motte.

simply pick up and carry forward to secure.

Look to see how others are secured, do it slowly, and you will have nothing to fear when mooring in the beautiful harbours of the French Mediterranean coast.

4 Cost of Living

In 1970 I wrote, 'at the present rate of exchange you can reckon on the franc being worth one shilling and sixpence'. Today it makes for easy price comparisons if you say that a ten franc note equals a pound. Thus a franc is now worth 10p, or what was two shillings . . .

How confusing it is to compare.

You go ashore at Le Havre and you see that prices seem to have increased since you were last in France. Some months later you go ashore at Southampton and you see that prices seem to have increased since you were last in England.

The notion dies hard that France is permanently more expensive to live in than England, more expensive that is, for every single thing. Many 'well informed' holidaymakers, having eaten regularly in restaurants and nibbled in pavement cafes, are absolutely inflexible about this, particularly their womenfolk, attracted by displays and prices of French clothes.

Restaurants and clothes are more expensive of course, but the real traveller will have observed that the trend of all round price increases started in France and has since been followed in England and other countries too.

Modest Budget For a long time now my wife and I have been spending many months of each year in France and the Mediterranean area. We manage quite well on a modest budget because we have to, surely the situation of the big majority of the French population.

If we cannot afford the best beef at twenty to twenty-eight francs a kilo we buy fish for five or a chicken for eight. Liver, fresh minced beef, chops and cutlets you can buy at favourable prices.

Bread is cheaper in France than in England. We consider it to

Cost of Living

Bread

be much superior and were surprised to meet a gentleman in Rouen who had filled his bilges with English wrapped bread of the blotting paper variety because he preferred it to the delectable baguette or flûte. Milk and eggs are no more expensive, nor margarine which I prefer anyhow to butter under the impression that it will not make me shipmates to so many fatty deposits.

We do fill our bilges with canteen-sized tins of coffee and tea; also baked beans because we are dull enough to prefer the British flavour, tins of minced beef for emergencies, corned beef because you never seem to get the same quality abroad, powdered milk for the rare times when we cannot find the real thing. If you are fond of jams and marmalade you would be wise to take supplies of your favourite brands.

Vegetables are plentiful and attractively displayed in markets everywhere but it always pays to compare prices.

French Markets

French markets are an absolute delight. To my mind the joint shopping expedition ashore is all part of the fascinating boating

French markets are an absolute delight.

experience. You have to eat so why not get the maximum pleasure out of the shopping and preparing?

We have met hundreds of boating couples, bronzed and dressed in any old clothes, shopping happily together in the markets, freely admitting that before their boating adventure they had never bought so much as a loaf together. From which you might infer that the cost of living, considered in relation to the boating life, acquires a new perspective. The price of cheese does not seem to matter so much when you are laughing at your loved one struggling to order a demi-kilo of potatoes and being served with apples instead.

You can buy food as cheaply in France if you accept that your diet will consist of different things. We have never made exact comparisons and, admittedly, in the consistently warmer weather we are happy to exist on salads, but we know that our food budget does not increase in France, despite the fact that a bottle of wine a day is a priority item.

Eating Ashore

In order to achieve this there are certain temptations that have to be resisted. Eating ashore is the first. It costs more to eat ashore in France than it does in England but perhaps a comparison is hardly valid because one is not really comparing the same commodity. We make the odd exception of course. We have been going to René in Marseille for years where, it so happens, the prix fixe menu has remained unchanged at ten francs. Only a few years ago ten francs was sixteen shillings and threepence in English money; today ten francs is a pound. René is still only getting his ten francs but you and I have to pay twenty per cent more.

Financial goblins are obviously to blame but now that the British are in the EEC, community control of food prices (which has eluded them for over fifteen years), will no doubt be achieved.

When you have finished your shopping and are tempted to stop for a beer or a coffee you must resist for you can have several onboard for the price of one that a waiter will bring you.

When you buy your baguette you must keep your eyes averted from the pâtisserie display if there is one, for a four inch temptation in pastry will cost you four times as much as the price of your bread.

Not all of the foods you need are sold in the open markets but there are supermarkets almost everywhere within walking distance of most harbours. Food actually available in the harbour shops is expensive because it is convenient. In the supermarkets

Cost of Living

language problems vanish and you can select up to the amount you can afford. When you get to Cannes or Baie des Anges or Nice do try to get a bus to Cap 3000, a supermarket at Cros-de-Cagnes with parking for three thousand five hundred cars, mostly full all of the time and never really crowded.

Corsican Prices

In Corsica prices are much the same as they are in France but you would not expect the same variety. Meat is inclined to be tough for some reason, possibly because the cattle get too much exercise, but fish are plentiful and good value. It is not easy to overcome one's typically British prejudice against unknown varieties but it is the key to cheaper living abroad.

You will find many nameless wines and cheeses in Corsica and it is interesting and economical to experiment. Corsican cheeses are made from the milk of sheep and goats in an enormous variety of tastes. Corsican wines are also produced in great variety; perversely we prefer the nameless local wines to the labelled brands and not only because they are available at a quarter of the price. Take your own bottle to be filled for real economy.

Harbour Dues

A big item in the budget of the cruising family on the French Mediterranean coast (but not in Corsica), will be in respect of harbour dues, but not so much out of season. In most ports east of the Rhône the season is considered to be from June to September. In the Languedoc-Roussillon the High Season is in July and August, the Season in April, May, June and September and the Low Season from October to March.

For a ten metre sloop the charge in the Languedoc-Roussillon ports varies from under a pound a day in the Low Season to over double in the High. But you could book a berth from April to September inclusive for about a hundred pounds and for the whole year for about twenty-five per cent more (less than half the cost of a marina berth in England).

East of the Rhône a ten metre sloop would pay 14F a day at Hyeres in summer and winter, 9F a day at St. Raphael in October to May, 20F a day in June and September, 22F a day in July and 24F in August. At Baie des Anges the daily charge varies from 9F to 23F, at Monaco a charge of 1F per gross ton covers a period of ten days. It has not been possible to get a selection of up to date charges for every harbour but I have provided as many as I can and they are shown on the individual harbour pages.

Somehow it is difficult to accept having to pay for a night's

French Mediterranean Harbours

lodging for one's boat and yet, I suppose, to even think on these lines is an admission of age. The days are long gone when you could come into a free harbour and more or less pick your spot on the quay; if all the yachts around now tried to do that you would not get in at all. So new marinas have been built at great expense and somebody has to pay for them.

Considering that you are berthing your boat on the most exciting coast in the world the charges must be considered reasonable. I have a friend who takes his caravan on the French Mediterranean coast and he tells me that the average charge per night is in the region of £1.50. The capital cost of creating a caravan site could not be a fraction of the expense of dredging harbours and harbour extensions, building new pontoons and laying water and electricity to them.

Diesel fuel is no more expensive than in England (but petrol is).

Comfortable Clothes

Old clothes are usually worn by yachtsmen (sometimes not altogether with the full approval of the second-in-command), because old clothes are comfortable and cruising is a comfortable life. But you must have sufficient, for you find that all clothing is very expensive in France. This applies particularly to childrens' clothes, even small items, so make sure that the wardrobe of any junior crew member is adequate.

The turquoise sea, the beauty, the sunshine . . . as the song says, the best things in life (and especially the French Mediterranean life), are free.

Arrangements for junior crew member.

Cost of Living

English—French Shopping Vocabulary

apple—*pomme*
apricot—*abricot*
artichoke—*artichaut*
asparagus—*asperges*
bacon—*lard*
baker—*boulangerie*
banana—*banane*
beef—*boeuf*
beefsteak—*bifteck* (well done—*bien cuit*; medium—*a point*; rare—*saignant*)
beer—*biere*
beetroot—*betterave*
blackcurrant—*cassis*
bread—*pain*
broccoli—*choux brocolis*
Brussels sprouts—*choux de Bruxelles*
butcher—*boucherie*
butter—*beurre*
cabbage—*chou*
can opener—*ouvre-boite*
carrot—*carrotte*
cauliflower—*choufleur*
celery—*céleri*
cheese—*fromage*
chemist—*pharmacie*
cherries—*cerises*
chicken—*poulet*
chop—*côte*
cocoa—*cacao*
cod—*morue*
coffee—*café*
confectioners—*confiserie*
crab—*crabe*
cream—*crème*
cucumber—*concombre*
cutlets—*côtelettes*
duck—*canard*
egg—*oeuf*
figs—*figues*
fish—*poisson*

fishmonger—*poissonnerie*
flour—*farine*
French beans—*haricots verts*
frogs—*grenouilles*
fruit—*fruit*
fruit shop—*fruiterie*
grape—*raisin*
grapefruit—*pamplemousse*
grocer—*epicerie*
haddock—*eglefin*
hake—*colin*
halibut—*flétan*
ham—*jambon*
herring—*hareng*
honey—*miel*
ice—*glace*
jam—*confiture*
kidney beans—*flageolets*
kidneys—*rognons*
lamb—*agneau*
lark—*alouette*
lemon—*citron*
lettuce—*laitue*
liver—*foie* (beef liver—*foie de boeuf*; calves' liver—*foie de veau*; lambs' liver—*foie d'agneau*)
lobster—*homard*
mackerel—*maquereau*
margarine—*margarine*
marrow—*moelle*
meat—*viande*
milk—*lait*
mushrooms—*champignons*
mussels—*moules*
mustard—*moutarde*
mutton—*mouton*
oil—*huile*
olive—*olive*
onion—*oignon*

orange—*orange*
oysters—*huîtres*
parsnip—*panais*
pastry shop—*pâtisserie*
peach—*pêche*
pear—*poire*
peas—*pois*
pineapple—*ananas*
plaice—*carrelet* or *plie*
plum—*prune*
pork—*porc*
potato—*pomme de terre*
prawns—*bouquets* or *crevettes*
rabbit—*lapin*
raspberry—*framboise*
rhubarb—*rhubarbe*
salmon—*saumon*
salt—*sel*
sausages—*saucissons*
slice—*tranche*
snails—*escargots*
sole—*sole*
soup—*potage*
spaghetti—*spaghetti*
spinach—*epinards*
strawberry—*fraise*
sugar—*sucre*
sweetbreads—*ris de veau*
tart—*tarte*
tea—*thé*
thrush—*grive*
tin—*boîte*
tomato—*tomate*
tripe—*tripes*
trout—*truite*
turbot—*turbot*
turnip—*navets*
veal—*veau*
vinegar—*vinaigre*
water—*eau*

5 Weather... and miscellaneous items

If the timing of your cruise to the French Mediterranean was wholly dictated by weather considerations you would come down through France in April, arriving in the Mediterranean at the end of that month or early May.

A cruise to the east would then be the best bet, spacing out the mainland ports and making for Corsica where the air is then fragrant with the scent of the maquis. Working your way back, seeing the French ports that you had passed by on your way east, you would be moving away from the sophisticated areas as they began to build up towards seasonal crowding in the harbours with the consequent higher charges.

You would arrive in the Languedoc-Roussillon when the threat of the mistral had diminished and could explore that end of the coast in leisurely fashion with room to spare almost guaranteed in most of the harbours.

If you were tempted to turn west too early, say in April, you would run the risk of encountering the mistral.

Mistral When the mistral comes it is no commonplace wind, no ordinary swayer of masts and sails and trees that you are accustomed to; it seems to have an actual voice resembling a flapping and huge tearing of cloth that it makes without any contact. You experience a giant push to your hull, a knock-down as sudden and physical as a blow from a whale. Screaming, incessant for days at a time and wholly demanding, the mistral lashes the sea into whirlwinds of white crests and waterspouts dancing insanely.

Winds arrive in the Mediterranean through gaps in the mountain ranges. The mistral is the NW wind that funnels down the Rhône valley and is so called because of its masterful nature.

Weather—and Miscellaneous Items

It is said that if the mistral has not arrived by 10.00 in summer (noon in winter), then it is not coming that day. When it does come it may last for two hours or two weeks but two days would be nearer the average duration.

As you would expect you get most mistrals in winter. In spring and autumn they occur less frequently and in summer hardly at all.

The further east you cruise along the Côte d'Azur the less likely you are to feel the effect of the mistral. The Gulf of Lions is the place to avoid at mistral times.

Weather forecasts keep you informed of the progress of the mistral. The French daily weather forecasts for mariners are rather difficult to follow unless you are a fluent linguist. They divide the coast into west and east with St. Raphael as the middle dividing line.

You need not worry unduly if you are unable to follow the radio weather forecasts because all French marinas have weather reports posted up twice a day. In some of the harbours you press the 'METEO' button by the Capitainerie to hear a pre-recorded forecast.

In Corsica the summer winds are usually pleasant and NW. You get rain in the spring but it is a beautiful season in which to enjoy the flowers and foliage of the island.

On page 8 of the *Mediterranean Pilot* you will find details of French weather signals, French storm signals and signals regulating entry and departure with which you must be familiar. A warning regarding tunny nets follows.

Public Holidays

1st January	New Year's Day
	Easter Monday
1st May	Labour Day
	Ascension Day
8th May	V.E. Day
	Whit Monday
14th July	Féte Nationale—Bastille Day
15th August	Assumption Day
1st November	All Saints' Day
11th November	Armistice Day
25th December	Christmas Day

in addition there are various local holidays.

French Mediterranean Harbours

Hire Cars There are numerous agencies in all towns. The temptation to hire a car is possibly strongest in Corsica, to see a lot of the island if time happens to be limited. There are agencies at all airports and steamer arrival points; a telephone call will bring a car alongside. You have to pay a deposit of about £25 and the 'value' that you do not use is returned to you. For a small car the charge is about £3 a day plus mileage. You must be in possession of a current driving licence and be over the age of 25.

To the charges mentioned might be added the cost of a bottle of Courvoisier to steady your nerves after driving around Corsican mountain roads.

Mail Can be sent to you c/o Poste Restante at any town and is reliable. A small charge is made on collection of your letters and proof of identity (passport), is usually required. Mail can also be addressed to you at any port c/o Harbour Master. In some harbours it is delivered onboard except on Sundays and public holidays.

Telephone is available at marina harbours.

Cats and Dogs can be brought into France provided that they have either:
(1) A certificate of origin and health, dated not earlier than three days before the animals journey, stating that it comes from a country where there has been no epidemic of rabies for three years and that it has spent at least six months in that country, or has been there since birth.
(2) A certificate of anti-rabies vaccination stating that the vaccination was given with a vaccine officially administered more than one month and less than six months before entry into France.

Puppies less than three months old and kittens less than six months old may be taken into France upon production of a veterinary certificate confirming age.

Weights and Measures

litres		gals
1	=	0,22
2	=	0,44
3	=	0,66
4	=	0,88
5	=	1,10
6	=	1,32
7	=	1,54
8	=	1,76
9	=	1,98
10	=	2,20
15	=	3,30
20	=	4,40
30	=	6,60
40	=	8,80
50	=	11,00
100	=	22,00

kms		miles
1	=	0,62
2	=	1,24
3	=	1,86
4	=	2,48
5	=	3,11
6	=	3,73
7	=	4,35
8	=	4,97
9	=	5,59
10	=	6,21
15	=	9,32
20	=	12,43
30	=	18,64
40	=	24,85
50	=	31,07
100	=	62,14

kgs		lbs
0,453	=	1
0,907	=	2
1,360	=	3
1,814	=	4
2,268	=	5
2,721	=	6
3,175	=	7
3,628	=	8
4,082	=	9
4,535	=	10

6 Harbours WEST of the Rhône (Languedoc-Roussillon)

Distances between harbours

Rhône to	Kms
Port Camargue	66
La Grande Motte	5
Carnon	10
Palavas	3
Sète	24
Cap d'Agde	18
Valras-Plage	21
Port la Nouvelle	28
Leucate-Barcarès	13
Port de Canet	8
St. Cyprien	8
Collioure	18
Port Vendres	3
Banyuls-sur-Mer	5
Cerbére	3

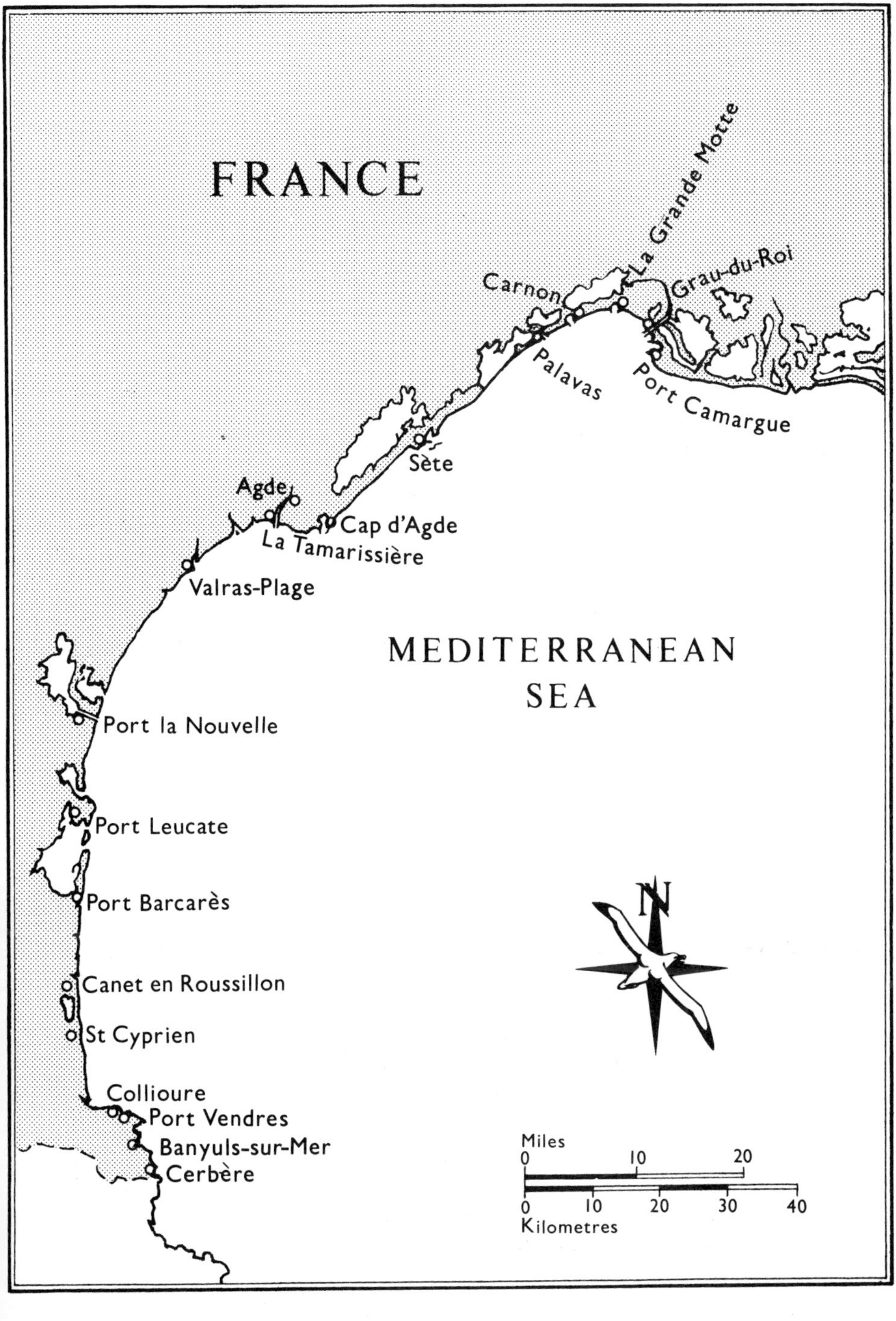
FRANCE
La Grande Motte
Grau-du-Roi
Carnon
Palavas
Port Camargue
Sète
Agde
Cap d'Agde
La Tamarissière
Valras-Plage
MEDITERRANEAN
SEA
Port la Nouvelle
Port Leucate
Port Barcarès
Canet en Roussillon
St Cyprien
Collioure
Port Vendres
Banyuls-sur-Mer
Cerbère
N
Miles
0
10
20
0
10
20
30
40
Kilometres

French Mediterranean Harbours

Rates for moorings in the yacht harbours of the Languedoc-Roussillon

LOW SEASON—October to March
SEASON—April, May, June and September
HIGH SEASON—July and August

Rate of Exchange:
£1.00 = 10.20 Fr.

Overall length in metres	Motor	Sail
C	6.50– 8.00	8.00– 9.50 metres
D	8.00– 9.50	9.50–11.00 metres
E	9.50–11.00	11.00–13.00 metres
F	11.00–13.00	13.00–15.00 metres

	PER DAY			PER WEEK			PER MONTH		
	Low season	season	High season	Low season	season	High season	Low season	season	High season
	£	£	£	£	£	£	£	£	£
C	0.70	1.40	1.70	4.00	7.00	8.50	14.00	24.50	29.40
D	0.80	1.70	2.00	4.80	8.50	10.00	16.80	29.70	35.50
E	1.00	2.00	2.50	6.00	10.30	12.40	21.00	36.20	43.50
F	1.20	2.50	3.00	7.30	13.00	15.40	25.80	44.00	52.20

	For the season from 1st April to 30th September	for the year
C	£100	£120
D	£120	£145
E	£145	£186
F	£175	£225

Port Camargue

Lat. 43° 31′ N
Long. 4° 7′ E

AVAILABLE: Water, fuel, repairs, hauling out, weather reports, chandlery, electricity.
MOORINGS: Apply Capitainerie, Port side entrance to basin.
CHARGES: see above.

The last, or first, of the harbours of the Languedoc-Roussillon depending upon your direction. Port Camargue is going to be a huge, many harbour complex with accommodation for 1,600 boats. Meanwhile the present harbour is splendid and there are

Port Camargue

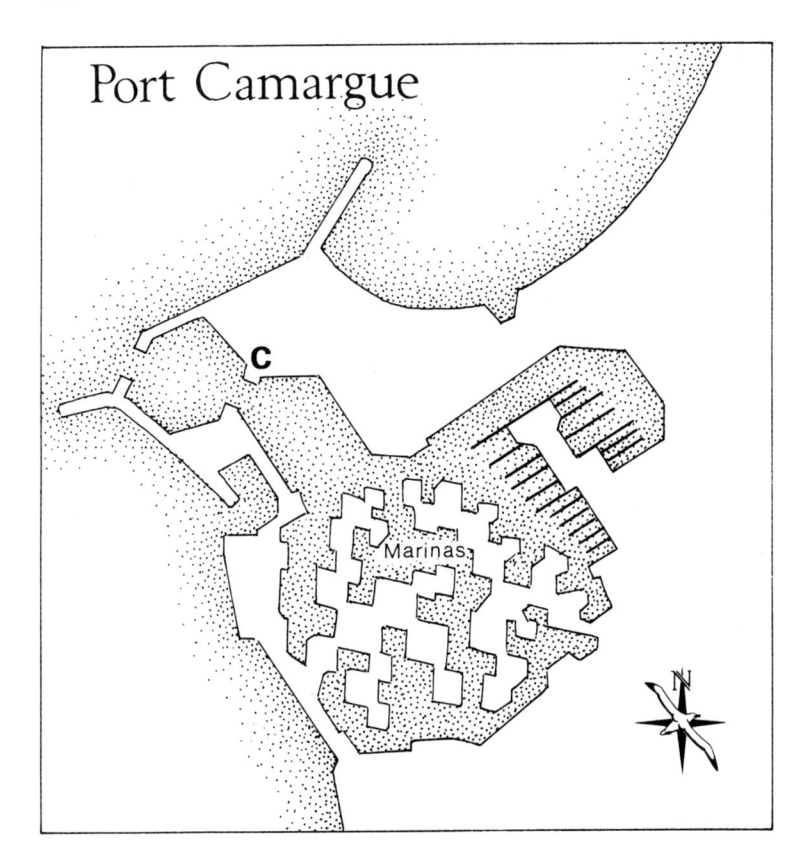

500 berths available at the moment.
Port Camargue is the least developed ashore. There are apartment blocks but no shops in the vicinity of the harbour, and outside of the harbour area there is nothing.

Grau-du-Roi

Lat. 43° 32′ N
Long. 4° 8′ E

AVAILABLE: facilities at Port Camargue.

Linked with Port Camargue, Grau-du-Roi is a picturesque old fishing village at the entrance to the canal leading to Aigues-Mortes about three miles away.
The waterway up to the swing bridge is monopolised by fishing boats and pleasure boats. Beyond the swing bridge is a

Grau-du-Roi yacht yard with a slip.
(continued)   Once past the swing bridge the waterway lies ahead to the towers of Aigues-Mortes seen in the distance. This waterway is used by boats kept at the convenient little harbour at Aigues-Mortes. Some voyagers to and from the inland waterways find this a convenient exit or entry to and from the Mediterranean but we seem to find Port St. Louis or Sète more convenient.

Grau-du-Roi.

La Grande Motte

Lat. 43° 34′ N
Long. 4° 5′ E

AVAILABLE: Water, fuel, repairs, hauling out, weather reports, chandlery, electricity.
MOORINGS: Apply Capitainerie. Starboard side, entrance quay to basin.
CHARGES: see page 60.

Grand indeed! This is the daddy (if not the Sugar Daddy), of all the Languedoc-Roussillon harbours.

Many moorings here have been taken up permanently and the British flag is more in evidence than at the other harbours on this coast.

The harbour facilities could not be bettered. Around the harbour a sophisticated little town has sprung up, gay and striking. The triangular blocks of flats at Grande Motte have been much publicised and property prices are a great deal more expensive than at other harbours in the region.

La Grand Motte

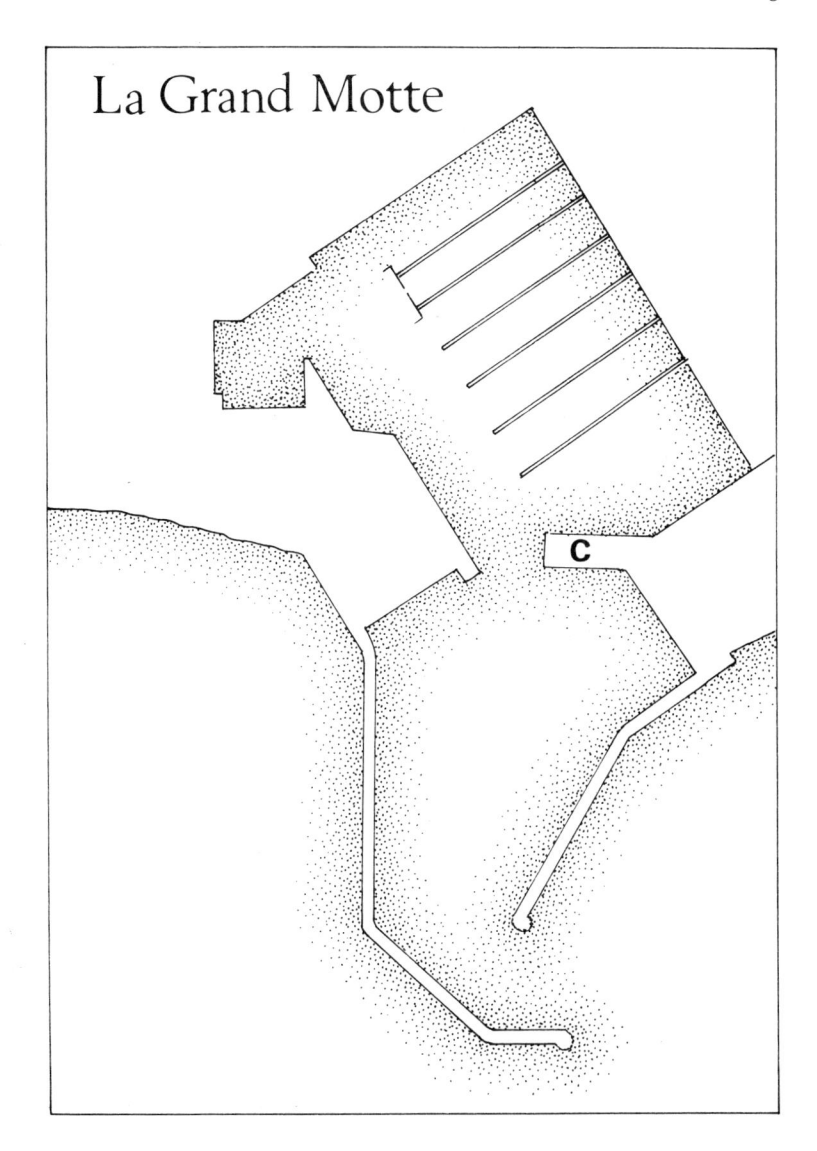

Carnon

Lat. 43° 31′ N
Long. 3° 58′ E

AVAILABLE: Water, fuel, repairs, weather reports, electricity.
MOORINGS: Apply Capitainerie, to starboard on entry.
CHARGES: see page 60.

Carnon
(continued)

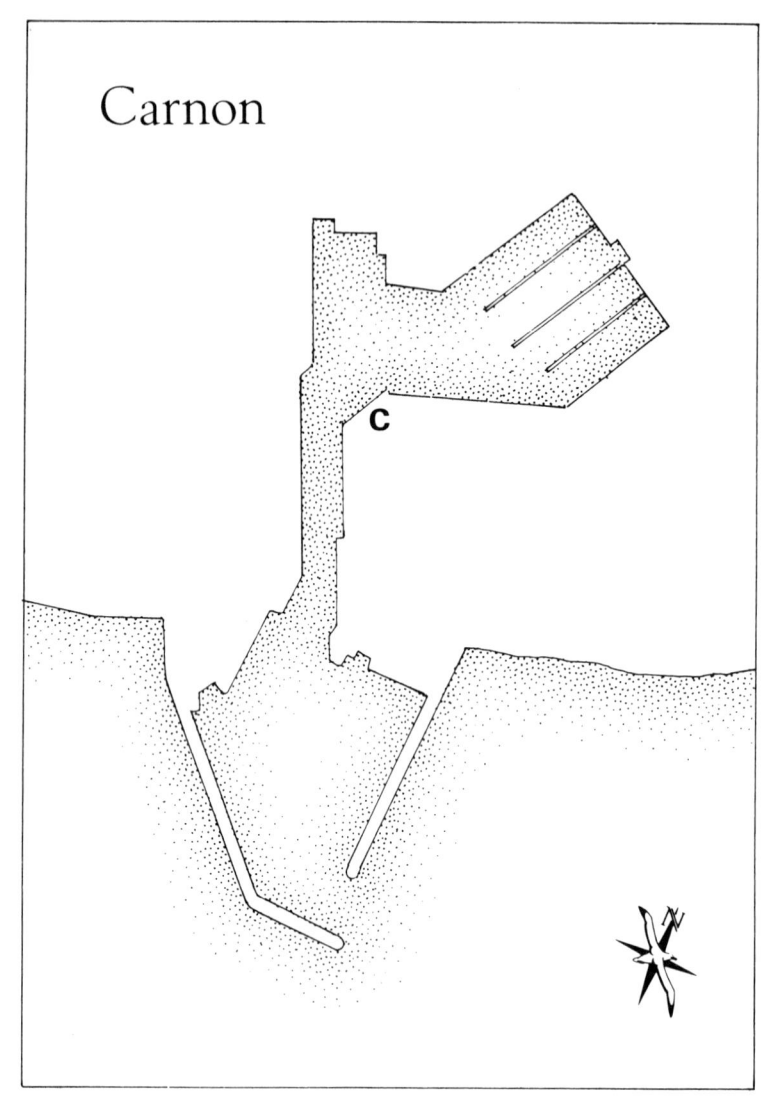

Carnon

The harbour is new and excellent; around are apartment blocks but there are shops at Carnon village within walking distance of the harbour.

Carnon is the nearest of the Languedoc-Roussillon harbours to an airport (Aéroport de Frejorgues), which is only six kilometres away and is the town airport of Montpellier, four kilometres

Carnon.

further on. You can fly from Gatwick to Montpellier in under three hours.

Palavas

Lat. 43° 32′ N
Long. 3° 56′ E

For small craft only; there is not much more than 1m depth in the river.

Palavas is on the banks of the River Lez and that part of the river below the bridge is taken up with mooring platforms for pleasure boats and fishing boats.

Above the bridge is the marina for small craft.

Palavas is a pleasant place ashore but of principal interest to yachtsmen for its prominent tower which enables you to fix the position of better harbours nearby. (For map see next page.)

Small boat marina at Palavas.

Port de Palavas
(continued)

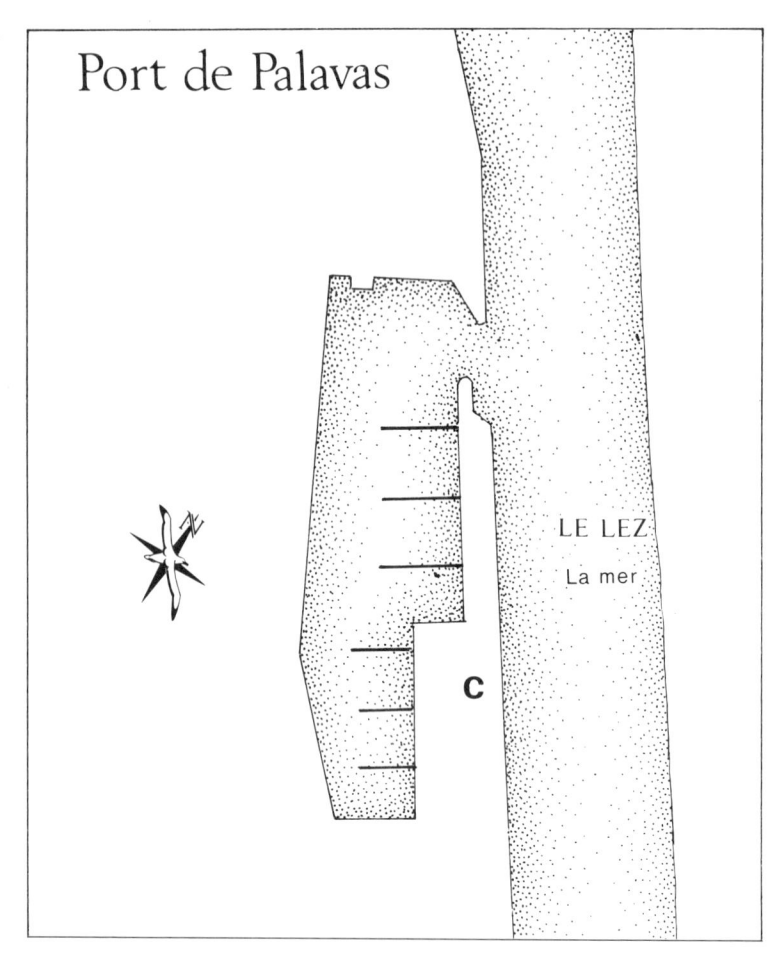

Port de Palavas

LE LEZ

La mer

C

Sète

Lat. 43° 24′ N
Long. 3° 42′ E

AVAILABLE: Water, fuel, repairs, hauling out, weather reports, chandlery.

MOORINGS: Apply Capitainerie on the shoreside quay of the yacht basin.

Principally a commercial port and fishing harbour Sète is best known, amongst yachtsmen at least, as one of the places where you 'come out' into the Mediterranean from the Rhône or Bordeaux—or where you prepare to 'go in' to the Canal du Midi

Harbours West of the Rhône

across the Etang du Thau. Barges take cargoes from here to far-a-way inland places but they have the power, lacking in most yachts, to get up the Rhône.

Rounding the outer breakwater you see the entrance to the harbour; you turn in here to port and prepare to moor stern-to in the yacht harbour. Approaching this yacht harbour you will see a waterway leading off to your right; the first sections are the fishing boat quays while the market is held by the round building on the corner.

We have known yachts with masts unstepped, or motor cruisers, lie very comfortably further up this waterway for quite

Port of Sète
Reproduced from British Admiralty Chart No. 1805 with the sanction of the Controller H.M. Stationery Office, and of the Hydrographer of the Navy.

Sète
(continued)

Sète.

long periods and a very pleasant place it is to be, with the town at the end of the gangway. We have also known of yachts being given the cold shoulder after only a short stay. The cut of your jib must have something to do with it.

Sète is a fascinating place. Every street seems to have a boat lined waterway alongside it; open air restaurants spill everywhere over the cobblestones, there is life and bustle and you are right in it. You can stroll up to the fish stalls and carry back your inexpensive supper, rocking gently in the wash of the fishing boats as they churn out to fetch you another meal.

The wind is no stranger to Sète, however, and this would appear to be its biggest disadvantage.

Water Festival 25th August.

Cap d'Agde

Lat. 43° 16′ N
Long. 3° 30′ E

AVAILABLE: Water, fuel, repairs, hauling out, weather reports, electricity.
MOORINGS: Apply Capitainerie on starboard quay ahead.
CHARGES: see page 60.

It is quite a long run in to the marina harbour visible ahead, all new and excellent. Three harbours will be developed here

Harbours West of the Rhône

Cap d' Agde

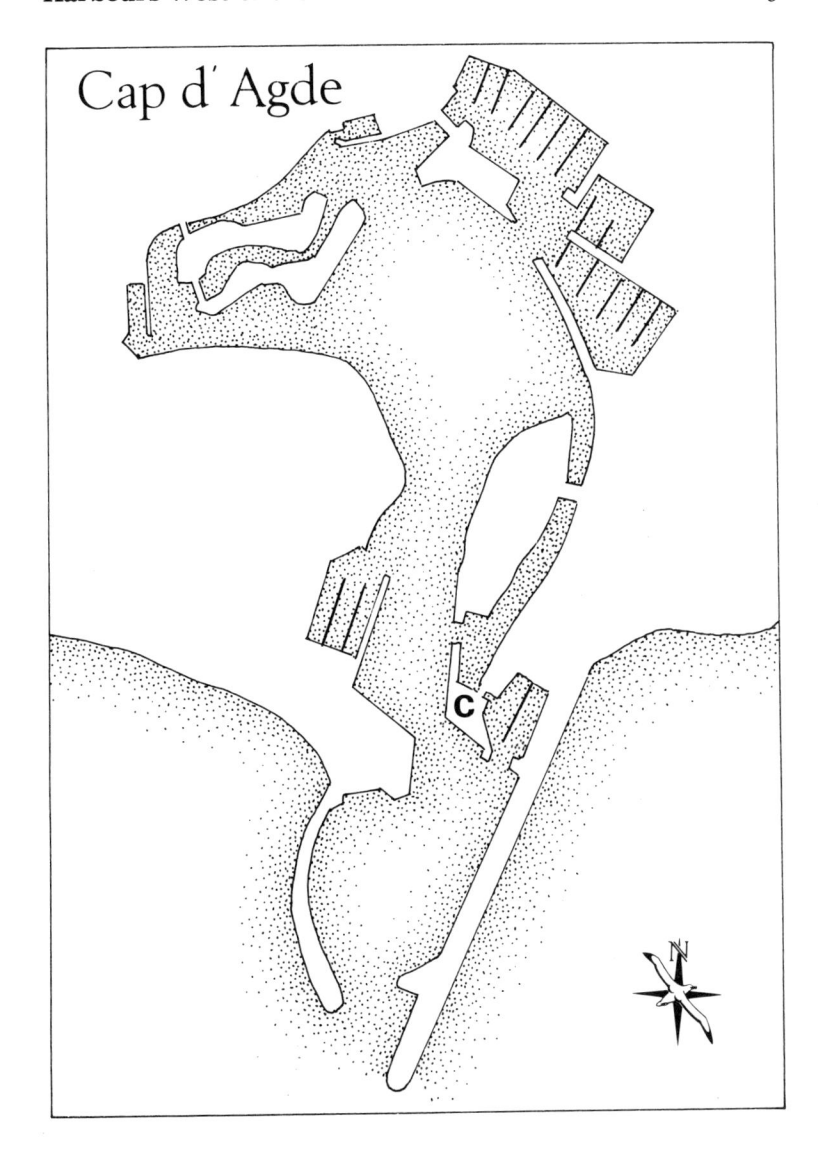

utilising the etang and accommodation for 1,000 boats is planned.
  Around the harbour are new apartment blocks, compact, in differing levels and colours, plus a good selection of shops. The architectural design has the higgledy-piggledeness of an old town yet all is brand new in brand new square shapes and bright colours. The resort is planned to extend as far as Pic Saint Loup

Cap d'Agde
(*continued*)

Cap d'Agde.

with an area for marina houses and accommodation altogether for 50,000 holidaymakers in an area of 1,500 acres around 200 acres of water.

The peninsula of Cap d'Agde is twenty-five kilometres from Beziers.

Agde

Lat. 43° 19′ N
Long. 3° 28′ E

AVAILABLE: Water, fuel.

An attractive old town four kilometres up the River Hérault and at one time a Greek seaport.

You can enter the river between the two jetties that extend seaward. At the mouth is La Tamarissière where you can secure to the quay to starboard and where there are a few shops ashore.

There is a good depth of water all the way up to the suspension bridge at Agde. Beyond, to the left, a small canal (in the middle of which is a low bridge), branches off to join the Canal du Midi.

The cathedral at Agde.

    Commercial vessels secure alongside the western bank of the river, yachts the other side.
    Agde is one of the oldest towns in France, built at the foot of Mont St. Loup, an extinct volcano from which the dark brown stone was taken to build the 12th century cathedral by the river.
    In the old quarter there is an interesting museum of folklore and archeology.

La Tamarissiere

    At the mouth of the River Hérault. Secure to quay to starboard. There are a few shops here.
                                   (See photo on next page.)

La Tamarissiere (*continued*)

La Tamarissiere at the mouth of the River Hérault.

Valras-Plage

Lat. 43° 15′ N
Long. 3° 18′ E

AVAILABLE: Water, fuel, repairs, weather reports, electricity.
MOORINGS: Apply Capitainerie, shoreside quay opposite entry.
CHARGES: see page 60.

At the mouth of the River Orb. On entry you will see yachts moored in the marina on your port side; stand by to make quite a sharp turn in to port through a rather narrow entrance, probably marked by two flags. The starboard end of the harbour

Valras-Plage.

Valras Plage

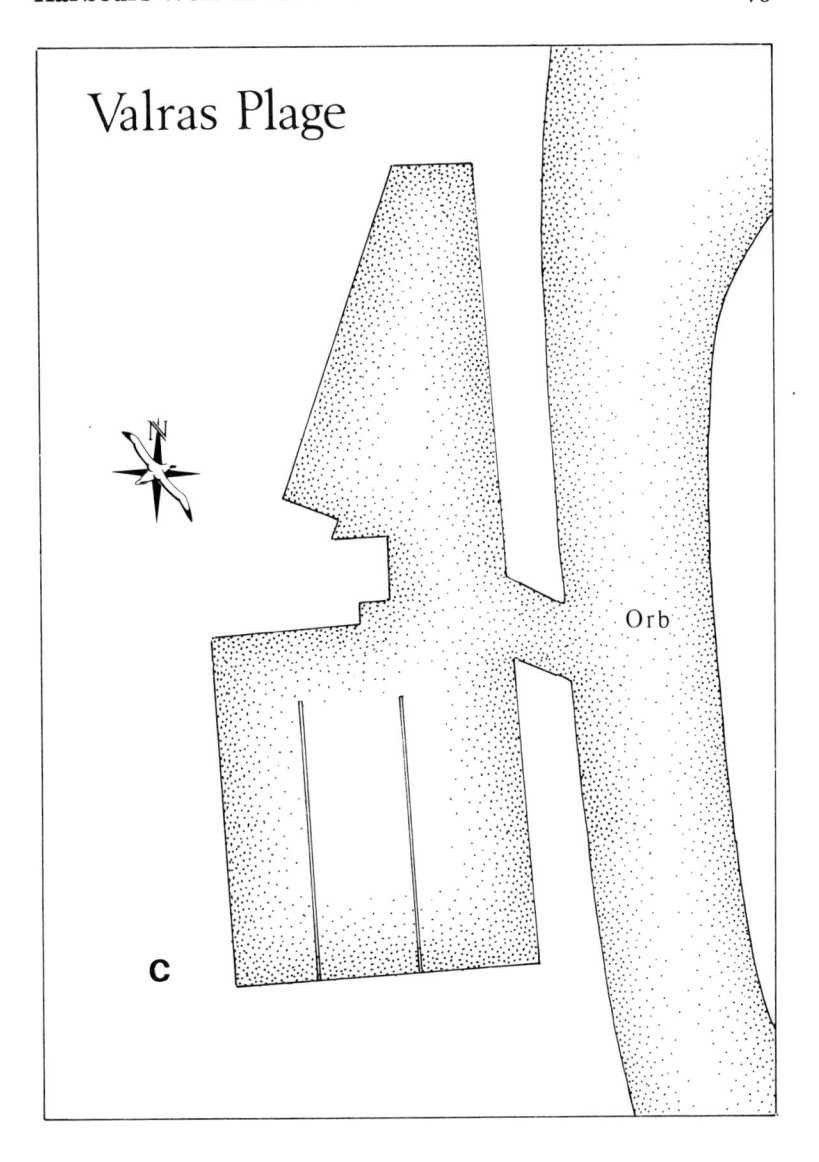

Orb

C

is occupied by fishing boats.
 You step ashore to quiet roads of quiet houses. The shops take a bit of finding but they are there.
 Further up the River Orb you see quite large yachts moored alongside the bank but the harbour is the appointed place for visitors and the facilities are excellent.

… French Mediterranean Harbours

Port la Nouvelle

Lat. $43° 1' N$
Long. $3° 4' E$

AVAILABLE: Water, fuel, repairs, hauling out, weather reports.
MOORINGS: Apply Capitainerie on the quay by yacht moorings.

This harbour is formed by a canal connecting the Etang du Sigean with the sea. The entry channel is easy to identify and extends for quite a long way, almost up to the road bridge where yachts will be seen tied up on your port hand. On your starboard side as you enter you will see quite large ships at the commercial quays; the fishing boats lie ahead on the same side.

From here you can proceed inland on this waterway to the Canal du Midi, turning left there for Bordeaux or right for the Rhône.

Masts may be stepped or unstepped from the bridge shown in the picture.

Ashore there are all shops available but Port la Nouvelle lacks charm.

Port la Nouvelle.

Port Leucate

C

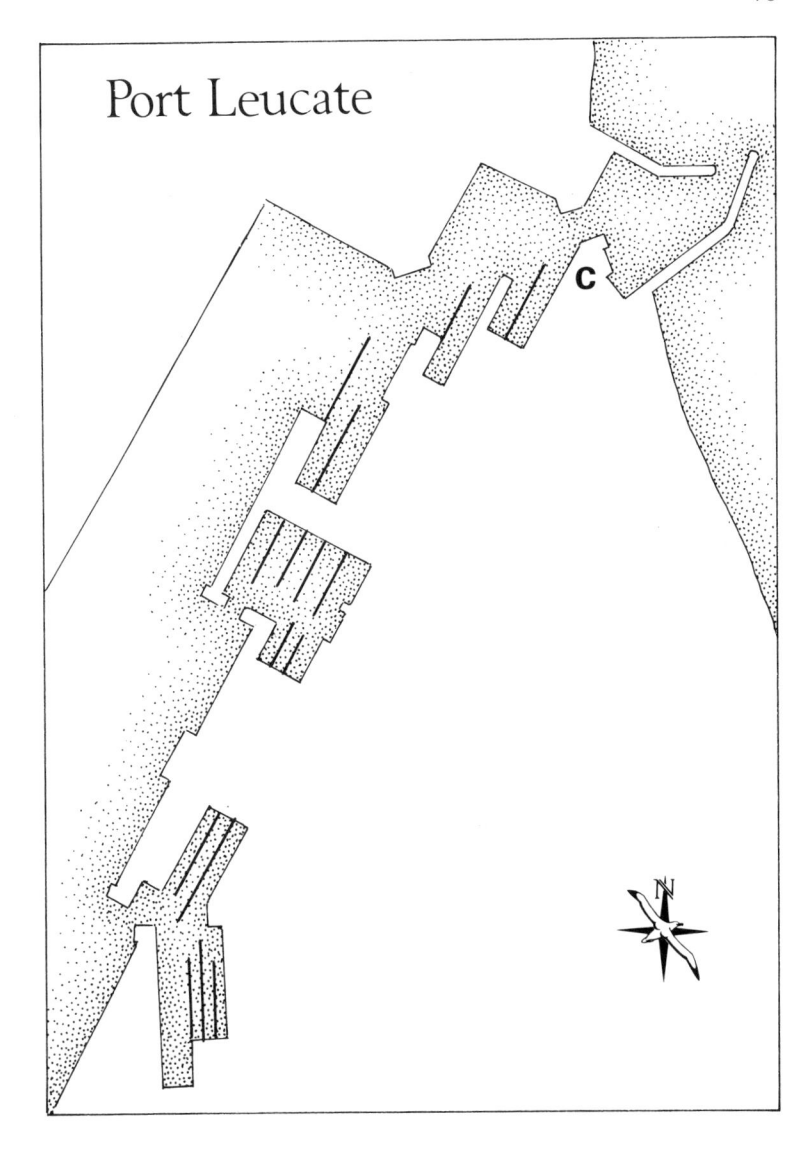

Port Leucate

Lat. 42° 52′ N
Long. 3° 3′ E

AVAILABLE: Water, fuel, repairs, hauling out, weather reports, electricity.
MOORINGS: Apply Capitainerie, port side, entry to basin.
CHARGES: see page 60. Continued on page 76.

Port Leucate.

Port Leucate will be the biggest of the Languedoc-Roussillon harbours with accommodation for 1,800 boats. It will extend through to the Etang de Leucate providing a choice of lake or sea sailing for boat owners there.

Of all these harbours it is the longest way in to Leucate, but markers indicate the channel. The first harbour to port is the boatyard with the lifting-out and launching-in pens below. Ahead, past white and gay coloured ultra modern residential box-like structures, turn in to port to the main marina.

Around you are gleaming apartments awaiting owners, the shells of shops awaiting trade and beyond, on the fringes and away . . . nothing, a desolate nothing.

Port Barcarès

Lat. 42° 48′ N
Long. 3° 3′ E

AVAILABLE: Water, fuel, repairs, hauling out, weather reports, electricity.
MOORINGS: Apply Capitainerie, starboard side, entry to basin.
CHARGES: see page 60.

Port Barcares

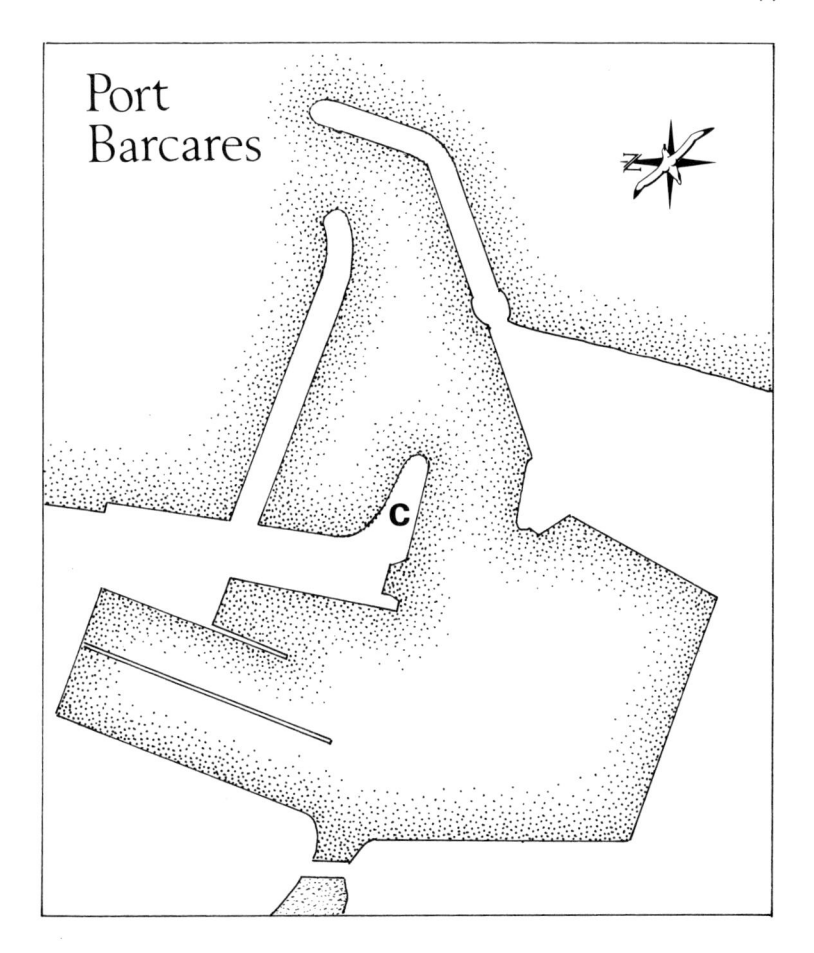

Turn in to starboard on entry and then to starboard again to the 200 mooring places.

Sitting in the cockpit it seems that you are surrounded by new apartment blocks; these also extend inland and away from the harbour area. There are also little islands, scarcely bigger than a football pitch, packed tight with new modern buildings, and buildings by the water's edge so that you can practically secure to your door knocker.

There will undoubtedly be all shopping facilities available one day in the vicinity of the port area; in fact it is planned that Barcarès will join up with Leucate to form the new holiday resort of Leucate-Barcarès.

French Mediterranean Harbours

Barcares.

Beyond the immediate vicinity of the harbour is a wilderness of scrub, dusty desolation relieved only by builders' trucks and dumpers. For prospective property owning boat owners or boat owning property owners this must be the best speculation on the shores of the Mediterranean.

Canet en Roussillon

Lat. $42° 42'$ N
Long. $3° 2'$ E

AVAILABLE: Water, fuel, repairs, hauling out, weather reports, electricity.
MOORINGS: Apply Capitainerie, port side, entry to basin.
CHARGES: see page 60.

Turning to starboard on entry you will see the harbour to starboard. The quay immediately to port is for fishing boats.

Canet en Roussillon.

Canet

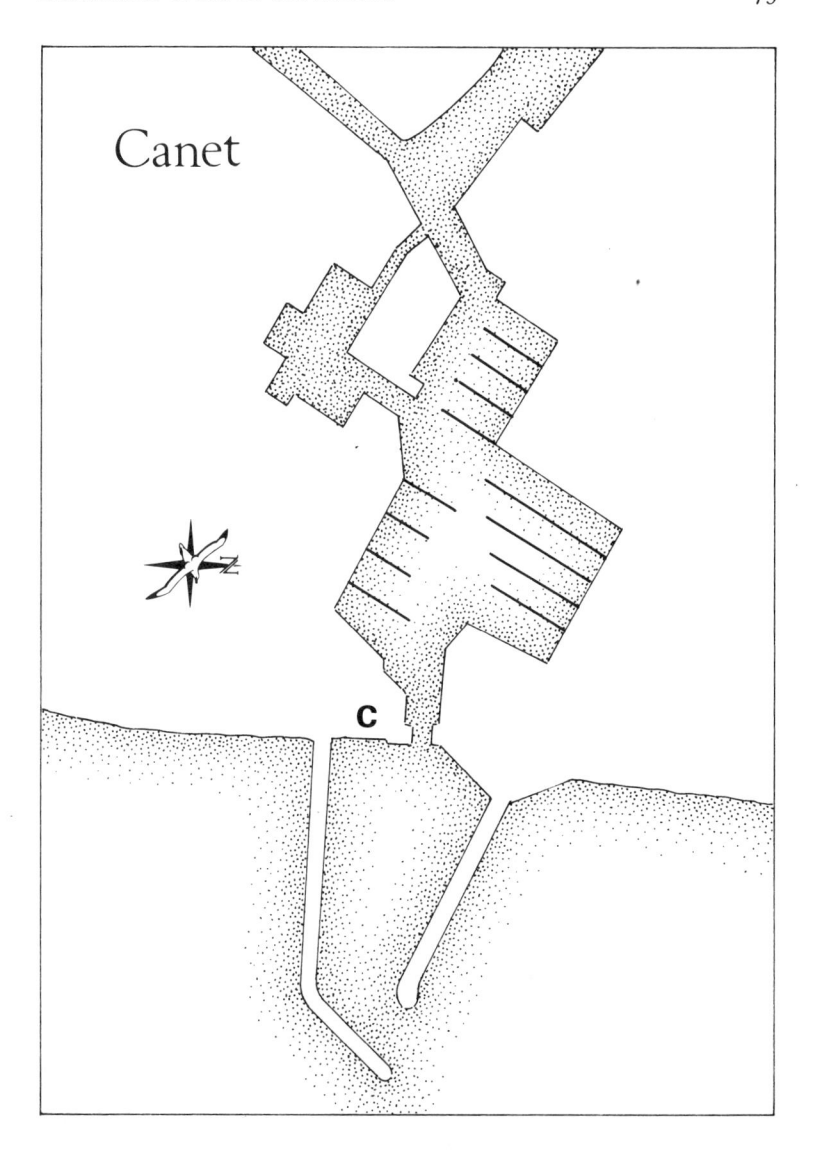

At the time of writing there are floating wooden pontoons but construction work is proceeding all around.

At least Canet has the advantage of being near to an existing town with all shops readily available. This is within easy walking distance of the harbour and is a charming little place.

With a long beach of fine sand Canet-Plage is quite a popular resort.

St. Cyprien

Lat. 42° 37′ N
Long. 3° 2′ E

AVAILABLE: Water, fuel, repairs, hauling out, weather reports, electricity.
MOORINGS: Apply Capitainerie on the fuel quay at entry.
CHARGES: see page 60.

An enormous new harbour, or rather two harbours. There are, or will be, 800 mooring places here with the usual arrangement of water and electricity to each berth.

Turn to starboard on entry. You will see fishing boats to starboard and the fuel berth in the outer harbour. The intention may be implemented to use the harbour to starboard for MOTOR craft and the harbour to port for SAIL craft, but the Capitainerie will direct as usual.

There is a selection of shops around the harbour, all new, but outside of this the car-less yachtsman is isolated. When you see the size of the vast car parks for boat owners you realise that perhaps you are not intended to sail a boat TO St. Cyprien; you

St. Cyprien.

St Cyprien

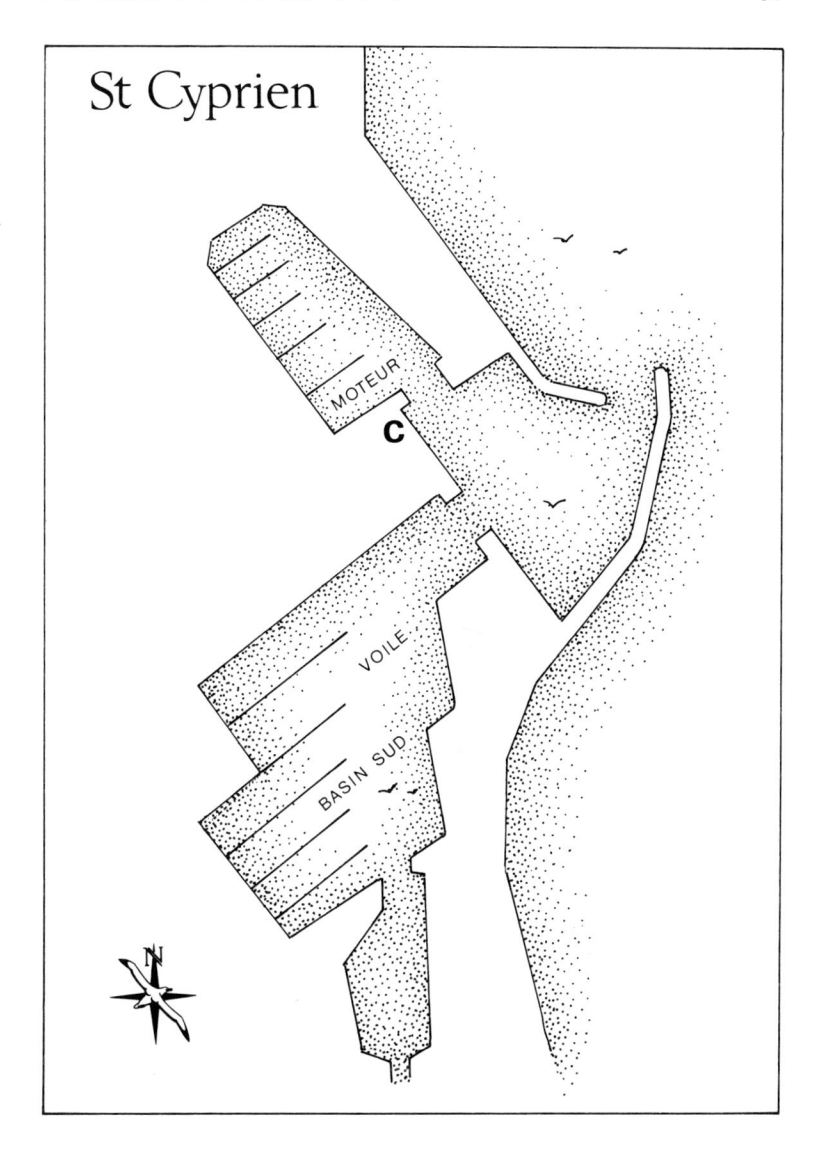

are expected to walk out of your apartment in Les Residences Calypso to your permanent mooring. Financially you could do a lot worse.

Eventually St. Cyprien will accommodate 24,000 holidaymakers around the 40 acres of harbour. At the moment most of the holiday activities and shops are at St. Cyprien-Plage.

Collioure

Lat. 42° 32′ N
Long. 3° 5′ E

AVAILABLE: Nothing in the harbour area but the town is adjacent.

A very small harbour. Officially there is room here for 30 yachts but entry should only be attempted in perfect weather conditions and then with the utmost caution.
　The approach scenery is very grand; with battlements and a tower you feel that you are steering for the front door of a castle. Round the end of the mole you turn to starboard across to the tiny harbour where colourful fishing boats may be taking up much of the available space.
　It is a pity that Collioure is not an easier place for a yacht to visit because ashore it is everyone's dream of a perfect Mediterranean harbour; pavement cafes with their colourful table cloths enlivening the quay, a castle background, narrow streets, charming little squares and shops of all kinds, painted by painters but not overwhelmed by tourists.
　But do not be tempted unless weather conditions are right and most certainly not if the wind is anywhere in the east.

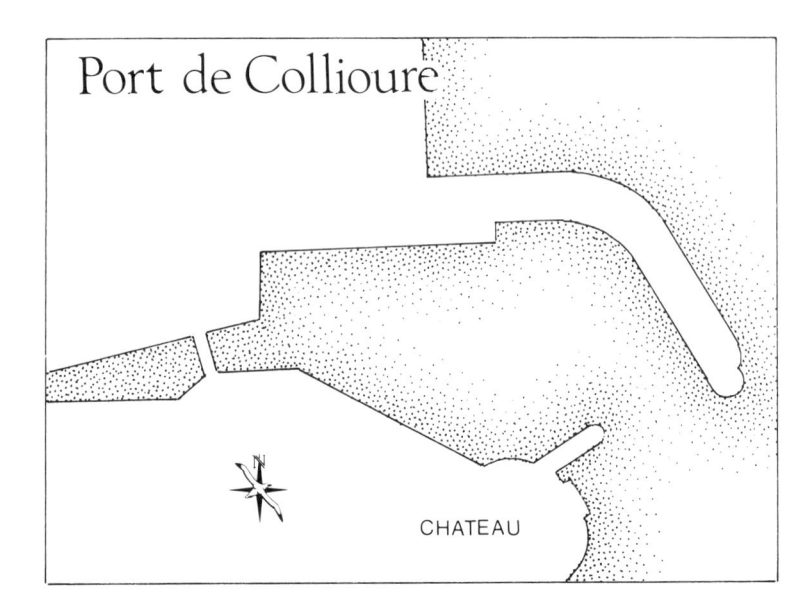

Port de Collioure

CHATEAU

Harbours West of the Rhône

Port de Collioure.

Port Vendres

Lat. $42° \ 31' \ N$
Long. $3° \ \ 7' \ E$

Port Vendres

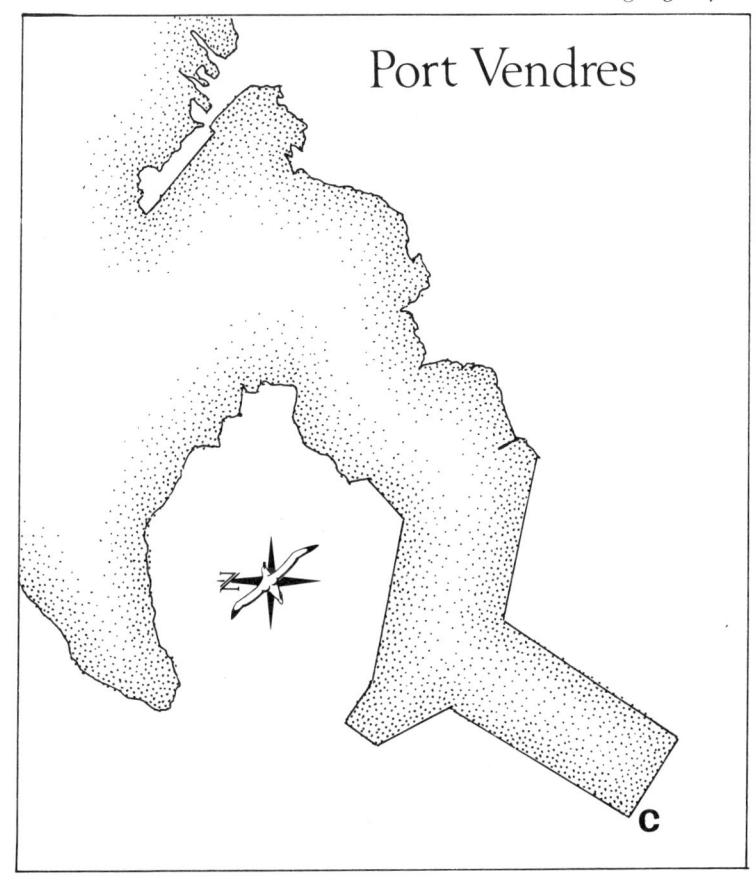

Port Vendres. There are now pontoon moorings.

Port Vendres AVAILABLE: Water, fuel, repairs, hauling out, weather
(continued) reports.
  MOORINGS: Apply Capitainerie at yacht marina end of harbour.

A splendid harbour and town. On entering you will see that the first quay ahead to port is for ships (mainly engaged in regular service to Algeria and Morrocco). To starboard the inset harbour is reserved for fishing boats, also the seaward end of the main quay to starboard. Further along this quay you can secure whilst enquiring about the moorings situation; the yacht pontoons are at the end of the harbour.

The attraction of Port Vendres is that the town is right on the quay. We have often waited in here for the weather to moderate; perhaps become impatient at the doleful forecast issued from the office on the quay, walked to the lighthouse at the point . . . to be convinced by the white caps and spray. At such times you will never find the fishermen going out and neither should you.

Port Vendres is the usual departure point from France going west and arrival point into France coming east; it is a very pleasant and convenient harbour.

Banyuls-sur-Mer

Lat. 42° 29′ N
Long. 3° 8′ E

AVAILABLE: Water, fuel, repairs, weather reports.
MOORINGS: Apply Capitainerie, on quay to starboard.
CHARGES: First day free, then:

Motor	Sail	\multicolumn{3}{c}{June—September}	\multicolumn{3}{c}{October—May}
		day	week	month	day	week	month
8 metres	10 metres	10 F	50 F	150 F	5 F	25 F	75 F
10 metres	12 metres	12 F	60 F	180 F	6 F	30 F	90 F
12 metres	14 metres	15 F	75 F	225 F	7 F	37 F	112 F
14 metres	16 metres	18 F	90 F	270 F	9 F	45 F	135 F

On rounding the red beacon you turn sharply to port in through a narrow entry when the whole of the marina-arranged harbour will be before you.

Ashore the narrow streets and shops are a pleasant walk away. Banyuls is a charming old place where Catalan folklore is maintained and you may be lucky enough to see traditional sardane dancing.

On the quay is the aquarium of the Laboratoire Arago containing interesting items of marine biology and diving equipment.

(Photo on page 84.)

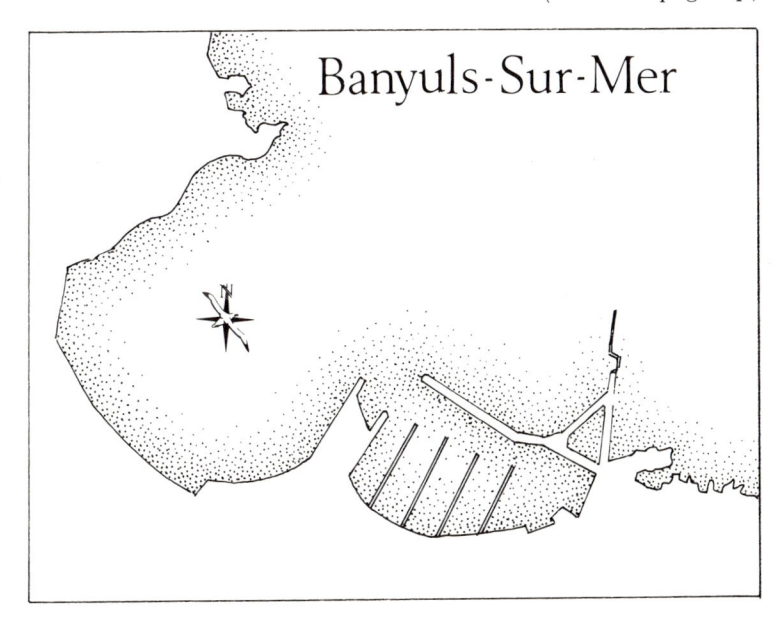

French Mediterranean Harbours

Banyuls-sur-Mer. Photo: Labo Bourguignon.

Cerbére

Lat. 42° 26′ N
Long. 3° 10′ E

4 kilometres from the Spanish frontier, the small bay of Cerbére proves an anchorage only. It is included here mainly because it is included in the development plans of the Languedoc-Roussillon complex.

On rowing ashore to the quay or to the beach a variety of shops will be found. Cerbére is an attractive place if somewhat dominated by the railway terminus of the frontier.

Harbours West of the Rhône

Cerbére, close to the Spanish frontier, offers an anchorage only, in a small bay.

7 Harbours EAST of the Rhône —(Côte d'Azur)

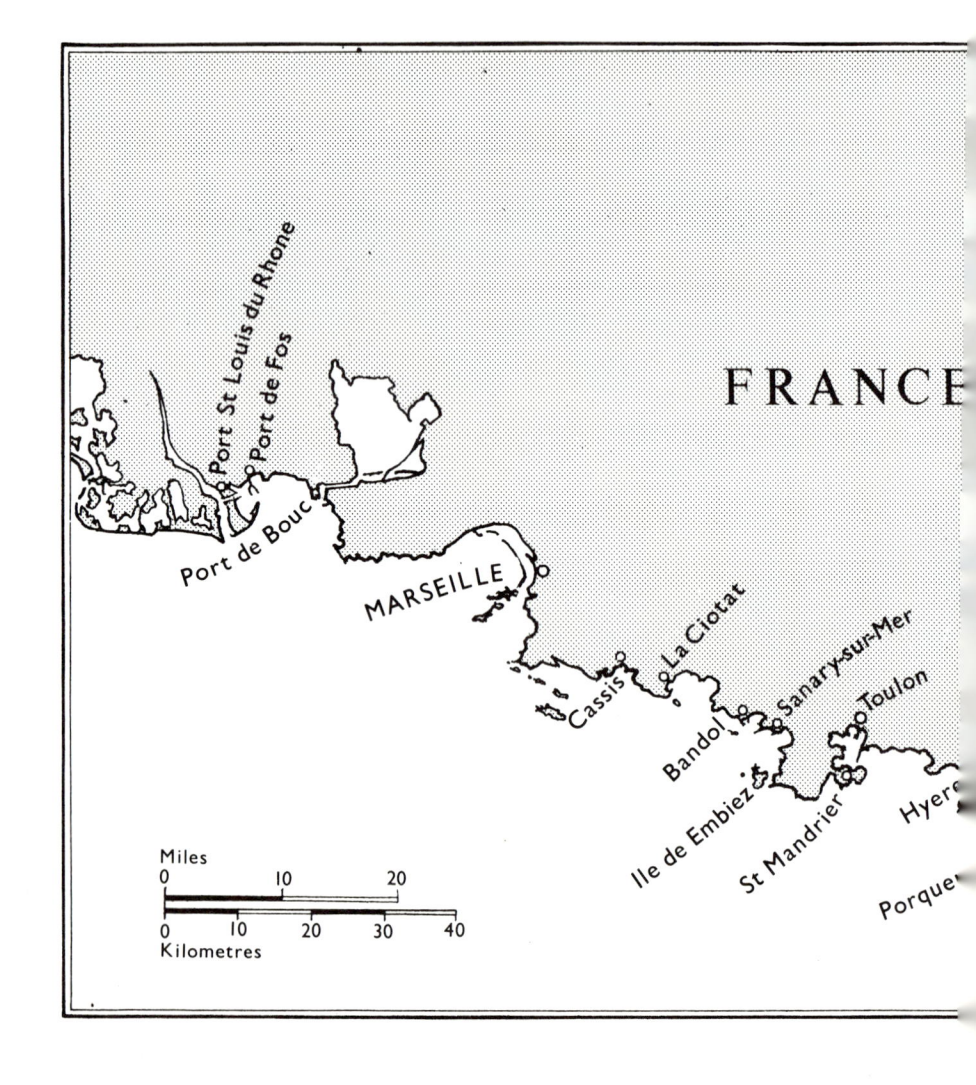

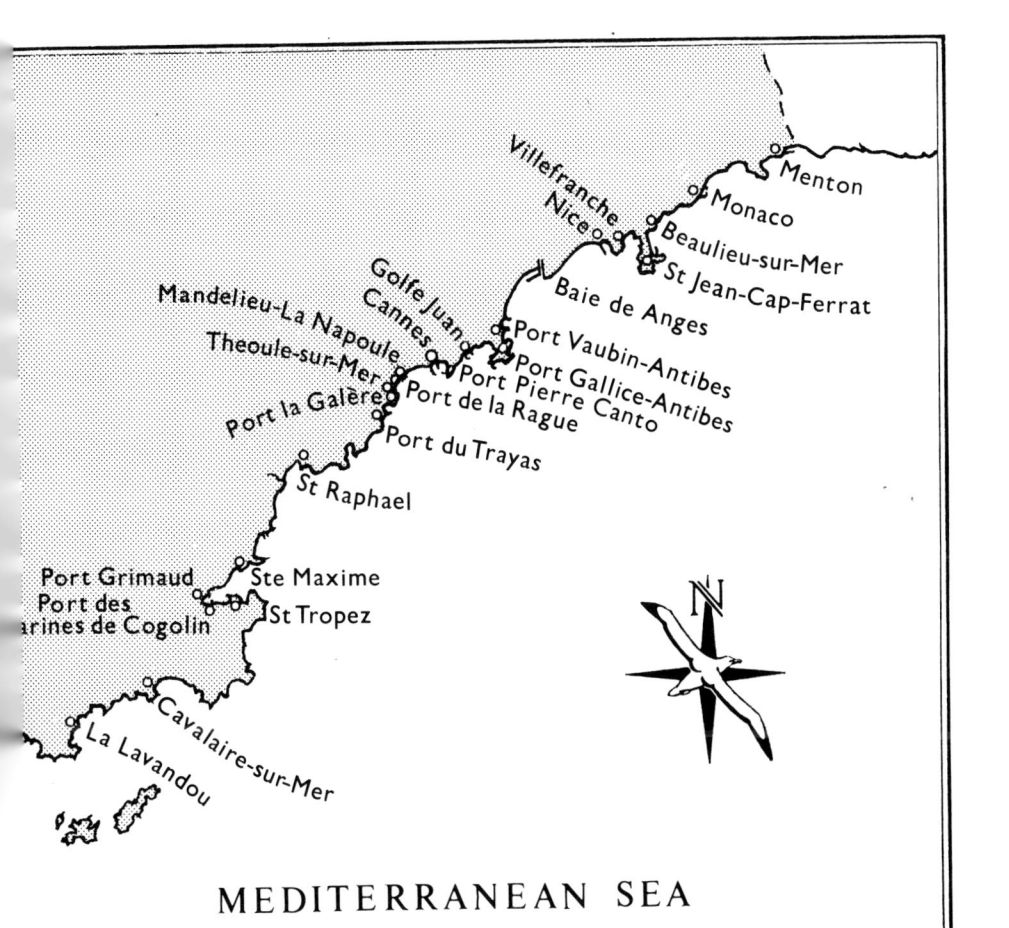

Menton
Monaco
Villefranche
Nice
Beaulieu-sur-Mer
St Jean-Cap-Ferrat
Golfe Juan
Cannes
Baie de Anges
Mandelieu-La Napoule
Port Vaubin-Antibes
Theoule-sur-Mer
Port Gallice-Antibes
Port la Galère
Port Pierre Canto
Port de la Rague
Port du Trayas
St Raphael
Port Grimaud
Ste Maxime
Port des
St Tropez
arines de Cogolin
Cavalaire-sur-Mer
La Lavandou

MEDITERRANEAN SEA

French Mediterranean Harbours

Distances between harbours

Rhône to	Kms
Marseille	43
Cassis	43
La Ciotat	11
Bandol	13
Sanary	5
Embiez	3
St. Mandrier	19

St. Mandrier to Toulon	5
St. Mandrier to Porquerolles	21

Hyeres	23
Le Lavandou	23
Cavalaire	13
St. Tropez	37
Les Marines de Cogolin	5
Port Grimaud	5
Ste. Maxime	6
St. Raphael	18
Port du Trayas	11
Port la Galere	5
Theoule	6
Port de la Rague	3
Port de Mandelieu—La Napoule	3
Cannes	6
Golfe-Juan	6
Port Gallice	5
Antibes	18
Baie des Anges	11
Nice	11
Villefranche	8
St. Jean-Cap-Ferrat	5
Beaulieu	5
Monaco	11
Menton	8

Port St. Louis du Rhône

Lat. $43° 23' N$
Long. $4° 49' E$

On one side of the lock gates is the Rhône, four miles up from the sea; on the other, the basin leading out to the Golfe de Fos and the sea.

Port St. Louis is the principal stop over port for craft coming from the inland waterways to the eastern part of the French Mediterranean. Since the Arles-Bouc canal is closed by the re-routeing of the canal at the Arles end, Port St. Louis is the first 'turn left' into the Mediterranean.

At the other end of the canal from Arles, Port de Fos is taking the place of Port de Bouc as the exit point of the canal in the Golfe de Fos. Even when the Arles—Fos canal is re-opened there will be no pleasure in it as a yachting waterway for it is being developed as a zone of heavy industry.

Somehow this seems to have made Port St. Louis more attractive although any such improvement must only be temporary because the whole area is scheduled for a new dock and industrial area link up with Port de Fos.

On making the sharp turn through $140°$ to port out of the Rhône you can secure to a good quay wall to starboard whilst waiting for the light controlled lock and bridge to let you into the basin.

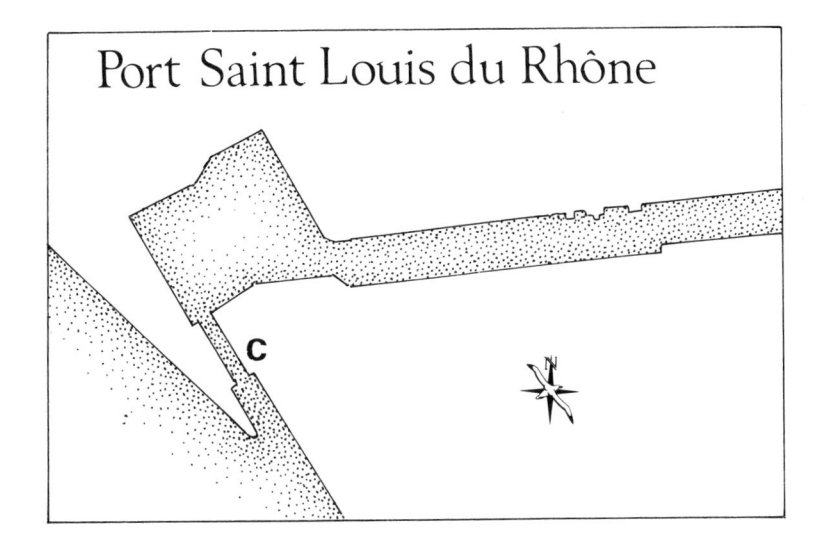

French Mediterranean Harbours

Port St. Louis
(*continued*)

Port St. Louis, out of the Rhône, on the left of the picture, turn up into the lock approach.

There is a boatyard here, a small chandlery and shops quite near.

Port de Fos

Lat. 43° 26′ N
Long. 4° 53′ E

A large area of industry and docks in course of construction. Of no interest or value to the cruising yachtsman at the moment. Admittedly it is the access to what is now called the Arles—Fos canal but with the Arles end shut off from entry to the Rhône (whilst the new lock approach is being completed), there is no point in enduring this canal unless you have business with the boatyard at Arles.

The Marseille Port Authority is developing Port de Fos for the reception and transit of petrol traffic and the port will be reserved for giant tankers.

Port de Bouc

Lat. 43° 24′ N
Long. 5° 0′ E

Port de Bouc is principally a commercial port at the seaward end of the Canal de Caronte which leads to the Etang du Berre. Shipyards are a prominent feature and the port is also of growing importance to the French petroleum industry—so keep a good look out for tankers on this part of the coast.

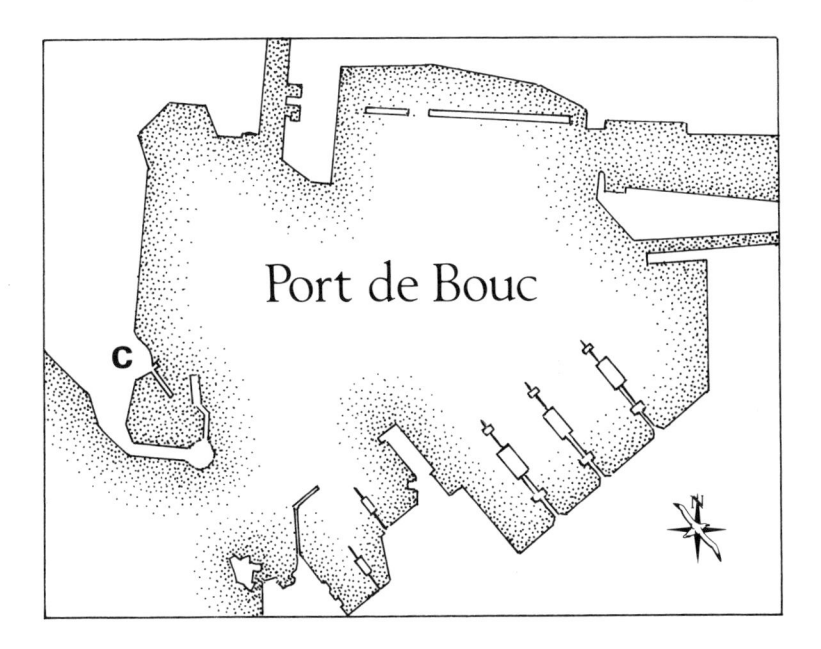

The square tower is the landmark to aim for; you turn in by it and immediately in to port round the small mole, at the end of which there may be tugs stationed.

It is a small yacht harbour in not very pleasant surroundings. There are shops ashore but the surroundings are semi-industrial. You may get a more pleasant berth in the entrance to what was the Arles—Bouc canal which lies—from the entrance tower— ahead and slightly to port, NOT the entrance to the waterway to starboard for this is the much used Canal de Caronte.

Port de Bouc.

Marseille

Lat. 43° 18′ N
Long. 5° 22′ E

AVAILABLE: Water, fuel, repairs, hauling out, weather reports, chandlery (probably the biggest selection on the coast), every facility is here.

MOORINGS: Apply Capitainerie to port immediately on entry.

CHARGES:

	June—September			October—May		
	day	week	month	day	week	month
9 tons	7 F	45 F	150 F	2 F	9 F	30 F
11/15 tons	10 F	60 F	200 F	2 F	12 F	40 F

Second city and principal seaport of France. Protected by a high breakwater the port area extends for over three miles and is made up of a series of communicating basins. Much of this has been rebuilt, having been destroyed in WW2.

For the yachtsman the Vieux Port is the place to make for, possibly the most lively rectangle of small boat activity in the world.

As you enter keep a look out for forceful fishing boats, fast motor yachts, indifferent ferries, hurrying tripper boats, sailing yachts (some sailing) drifting around looking for a mooring.

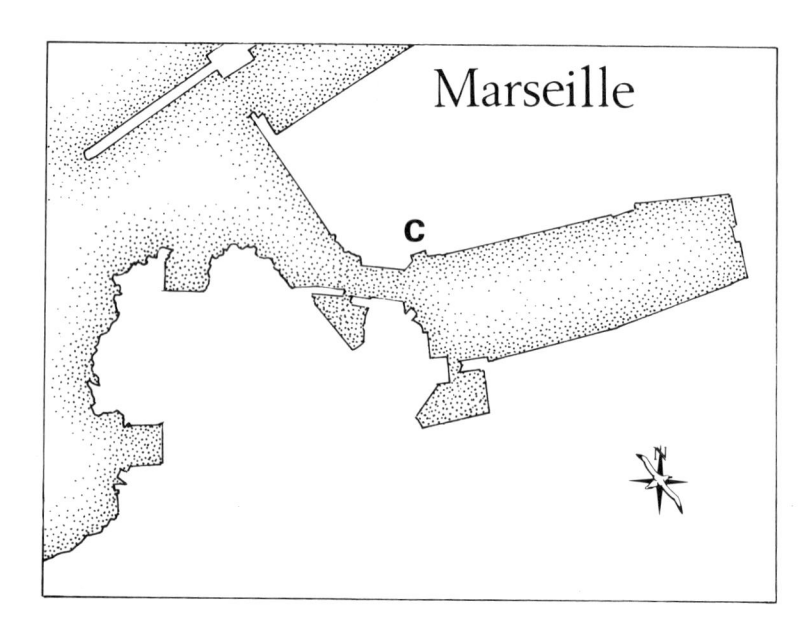

Marseille.

There is, of course, the yacht harbour at MOURREPIANE down behind the big ship harbours, railway sidings, storage tanks and the dock area generally, but it is a long and tedious distance away. The Vieux Port is much preferred in terms of interest and convenience.

Although noisy, bustling, somewhat intimidating at first you simply must go in to Marseille if only for the experience. At every moment there is something going on; you hardly have a moment to put the kettle on or to light your pipe without being called to come 'Quickly You Must See This?'

All around you (and it is a long, long walk around you but there are two ferries crossing the Vieux Port continuously), are pavement cafes, shops, traffic, promenades, people. Everything you could want for yourself or for your boat is here. In the chandlers' shops, with old fashioned floors and display units stretching back into the gloom, you see well thumbed boxes of everything, familiar and unfamiliar names. You have only to ask for your favourite paint, varnish, anything and it is produced immediately.

Leading up and away from the Vieux Port is La Canebière,

Marseille one of the best known streets in the world, with beautiful shops,
(*continued*) crowded cafes, hotels.

TO SEE: The view from the Basilica of Notre-Dame (go up by lift).
Marseilles Maritime Museum; history of Marseille and of French Navy—ship models, paintings, maps.
Musée des Docks Romains; Huge jars, pottery, history of Marseille in Roman times.
Musée du Vieux Marseilles; many exhibits of nautical interest.

Marseille.

Cassis

Lat. $43° \; 13' \; N$
Long. $5° \; 32' \; E$

AVAILABLE: Water, fuel, repairs, hauling out, weather reports.
MOORINGS: Apply Capitainerie to port immediately on entry.

The rock formations, the calanques, form a dramatic background setting; reaching heights of over 500ft they make a striking contrast with the deep blue sea that is intensely blue here.
Cassis is a sheltered and pleasant small port and fishing village in a crescent shaped bay. Coming in round the end of the mole you will see the harbour ahead with the small boatyard and fuel pumps on the starboard side.
It is a fairly tight fit for a large yacht and you sometimes get quite a strong eddy off the end of the mole. But once secured it is a most attractive place to be in with all shops around the

Harbours East of the Rhône

Cassis.

harbour, plus the type of pavement restaurants that you imagine in your dreams of the Mediterranean.

Despite the encroachment of yachting interests this is a real fishing port and the fish here are said to be very good. If you happen to be here on 29th June you will see the fishermen celebrating St. Peter's day with all sorts of nautical antics.

You will, no doubt, be familiar with Cassis white wine, particularly the blanc-de-blanc.

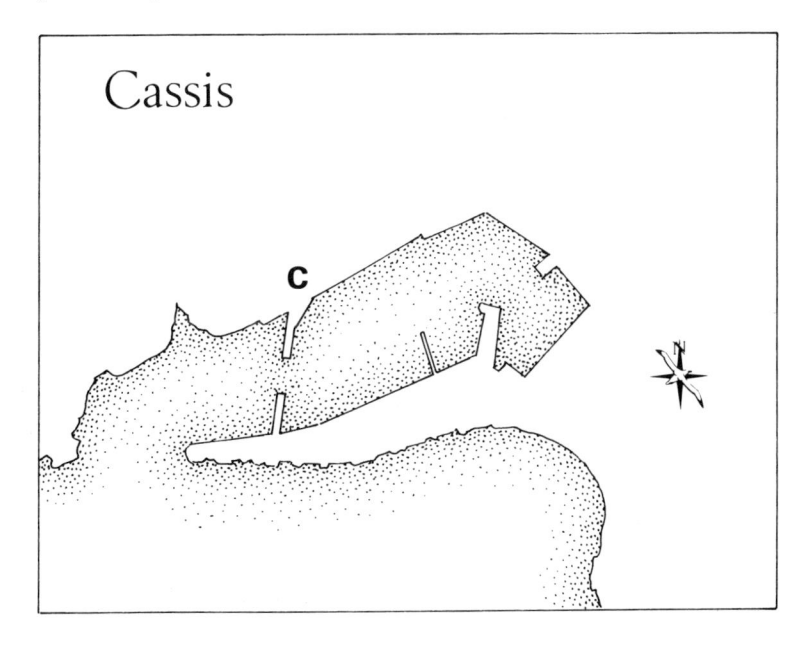

La Ciotat

Lat. 43° 11′ N
Long. 5° 37′ E

AVAILABLE: Water, fuel, repairs, hauling out, weather reports, electricity, big shipyard facilities.

MOORINGS: Apply Bureau du Port on quay between Bassin des Capucins and Bassin Bérouard.

A ship building town set in a beautiful bay.

Rounding the end of the outer mole you will see slightly to port ahead the Vieux Port, unmistakable with huge cranes attending the ships under construction. You may see yachts moored at the end of this harbour but the yacht harbour is along to starboard; whilst looking ahead at the Vieux Port, probably in astonishment at the size of the ships you see there, you may be surprised to learn that they are actually *launched* in this harbour.

Vieux Port, La Ciotat   Photo: A. Poncat.

Harbours East of the Rhône

La Ciotat

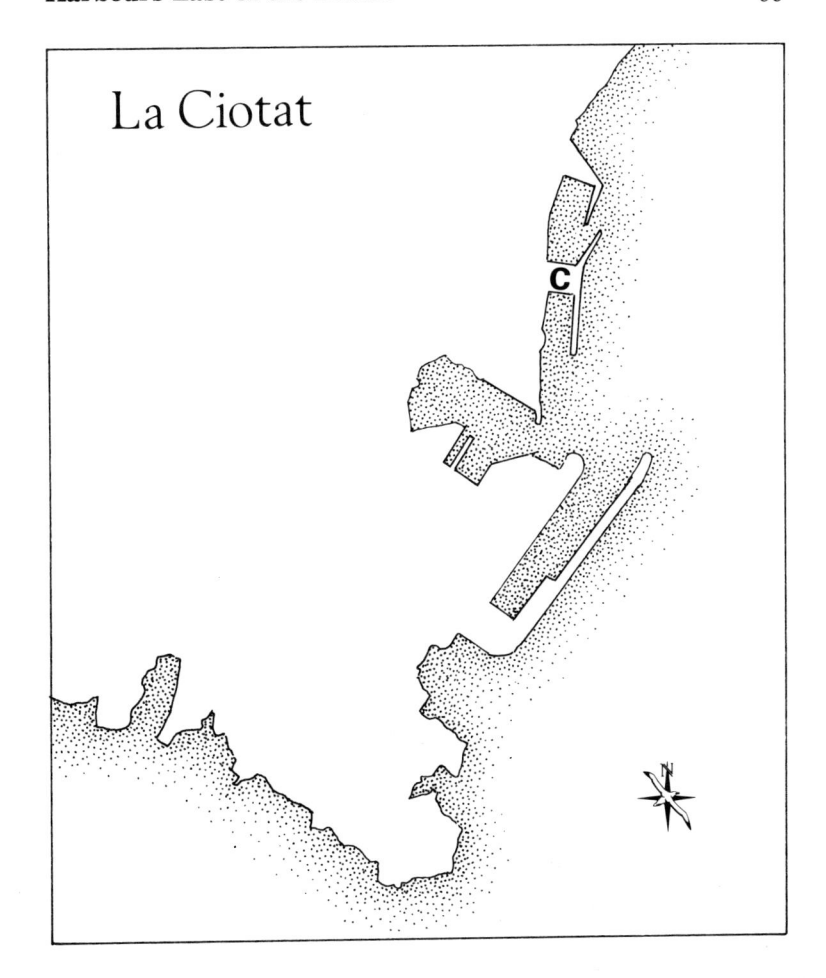

To reach the yacht harbour carry on past the first small harbour that you see to port and turn in sharply to port around the next mole; the Bureau du Port will then be ahead.

There are all shops, facilities and night life near to the harbour in La Ciotat. Imagine sitting at a pavement cafe and watching ships being built; rather like sitting in a hot Clydebank with palm trees. But the shipbuilding noises are not so intrusive in the yacht harbour. And as you proceed along the coast to the places where industry does not intrude you will no doubt reflect that it is better sometimes to stay in a yacht harbour with an industrial town adjacent than to stay in a yacht harbour with no town at all.

Bandol

Lat. 43° 8′ N
Long. 5° 45′ E

AVAILABLE: Water, fuel, hauling out, weather reports, electricity.
MOORINGS: Apply Capitainerie across to port on the shoreside quay.
CHARGES:

	June—September			October—May		
	day	week	month	day	week	month
10 metres	20 F	40 F	280 F	20 F	40 F	280 F

The yacht moorings are being extended here making Bandol one of the most attractive ports of call. It is situated in a sheltered bay and in surroundings of great beauty.

This is a large yacht harbour fringed with tree-lined promenades, behind which are narrow streets and a wide selection of attractive shops. There is a market within view of your mooring.

It is a charming and fashionable little resort with sandy beaches only a short walk away.

The harbour of the Ile de Bendor, a short sail from Bandol, is classed as a Port privé, but tens of thousands of trippers flock to the island in the motor-boat trips from Bandol attracted by the beaches, zoo, theatre and wine museum.

Bandol.

Sanary-sur-Mer

Lat. $43° \ 7' \ N$
Long. $5° \ 48' \ E$

AVAILABLE: Water, fuel, weather reports, electricity.
MOORINGS: Apply Capitainerie immediately to port on entry.

Tucked away in the corner of the bay Sanary is well sheltered and attractively situated against a background of wooded hills; thus protected from the mistral it is a popular winter resort.

Pontoon moorings have been built and more are being added.

Sanary is another 'dream' Mediterranean harbour, clean, only a few steps ashore to the palm tree lined promenade, with narrow streets, and attractive shops. It is a charming little town, practically unspoiled.

Sanary.

Ile des Embiez

Lat. 43° 5′ N
Long. 5° 47′ E

AVAILABLE: Water, fuel, repairs, weather reports, electricity.
MOORINGS: Apply Capitainerie on quay to port on entry, just past ferry quay.
CHARGES: *Day:* 16.80 F
Month: 13 F per metre overall length
Year: 11 F monthly rate per metre overall length, payable six months in advance.

Your chart will show you the way past the various obstructions; as you approach the harbour look for a double row of small markers to lead you in. Keep a look out for ferries that may appear from the quay on your port side; the pontoon moorings in this splendid large harbour will be before you and it is likely that you will see many yachts, and large yachts, here.

There is a small boatyard. Although Embiez is only a little island there are all facilities within a few steps of the moorings; quite a select bar and adjacent supermarket in which a surprising range of marine gear and clothing is displayed. There is also a pâtisserie and a restaurant.

Embiez.

Les Embiez

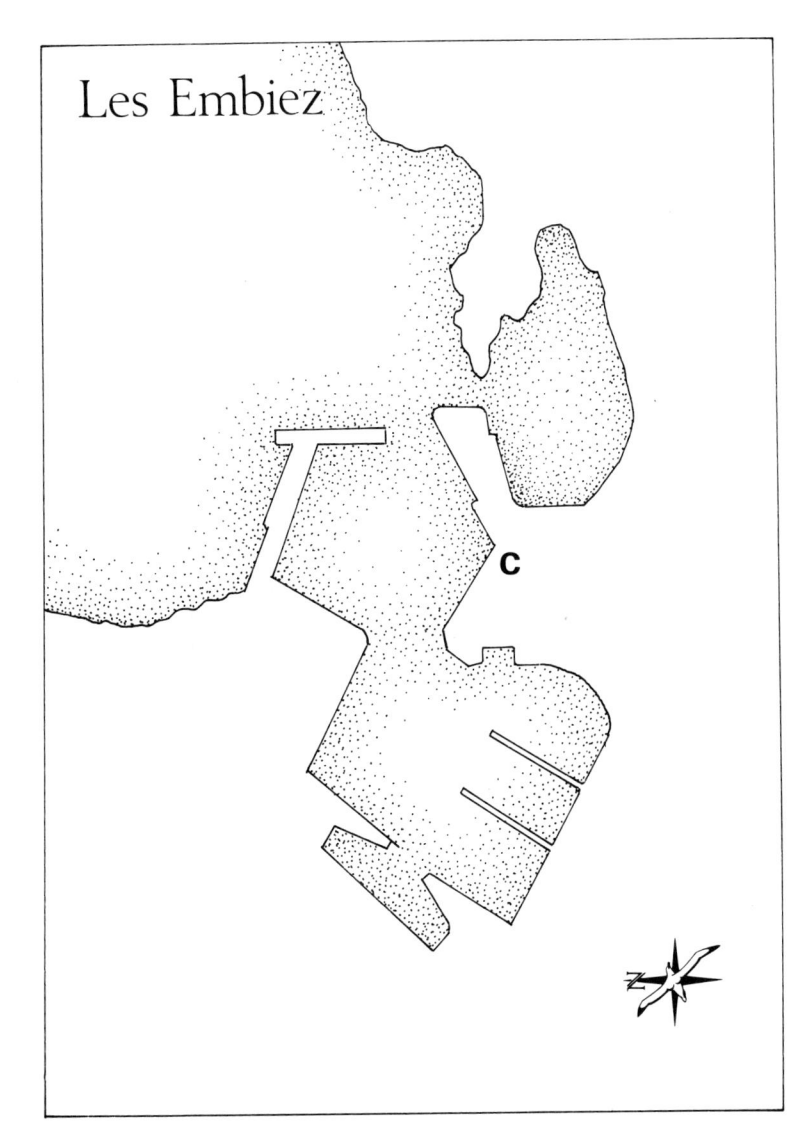

You can wander amongst fir trees and peacocks to unspoilt coves; the island is practically untouched by building development except for the harbour facilities.

The museum of the Observatoire de la Mer (with which Alain Bombard is associated), is well worth a visit.

It is, of course, an island but a ferry runs frequently to the mainland, too frequently you may consider in the 'tripper' season.

St. Mandrier

Lat. 43° 5′ N
Long. 5° 56′ E

AVAILABLE: Water, fuel, weather reports, electricity.
MOORINGS: Apply Capitainerie at the root of the starboard mole on entry.
CHARGES:

metres	October—April day	week	month	May, June September day	week	month	July and August day	week	month
21–31	9 F	54 F	216 F	11 F	66 F	264 F	16 F	96 F	384 F
31–40	10 F	60 F	240 F	13 F	78 F	312 F	19 F	114 F	456 F
41–50	11 F	66 F	264 F	15 F	90 F	360 F	22 F	132 F	528 F
51–70	12 F	72 F	288 F	17 F	102 F	408 F	25 F	150 F	600 F

A wide expanse of harbour. Coming up into the bay, at the head of which is Toulon, you see the central breakwater ahead and the smaller mole to port; just after passing this turn in to port. It is likely that warships will be moored here and you leave them to port, after which the entrance to the spacious yacht harbour will be seen ahead.

With mostly pontoon moorings this is a friendly sort of harbour

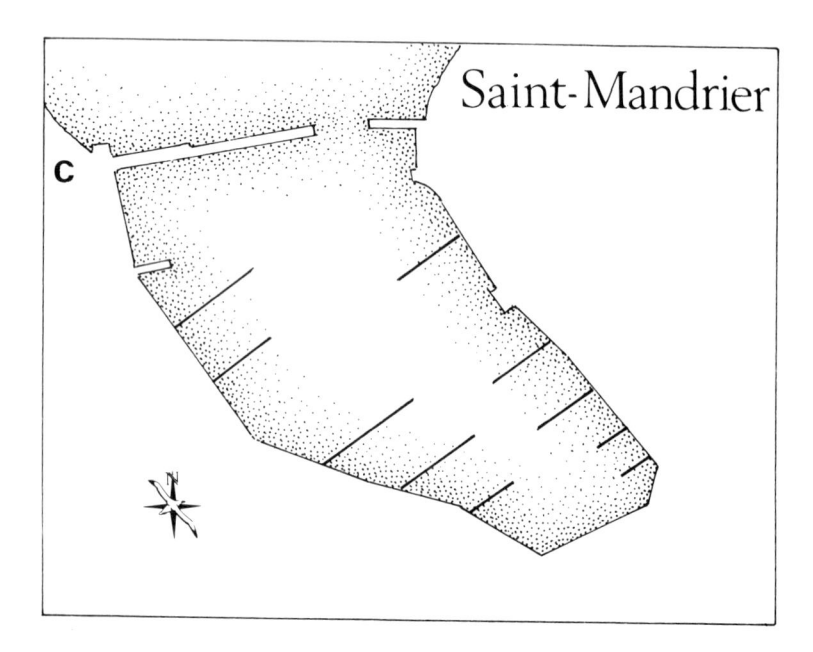

St. Mandrier.

and the surroundings are pleasant with shops of all sorts in view. In fact it is the sort of mooring that you find yourself staying in longer than you intended.

There are bus services to Toulon so that you can consider visiting the city in this way instead of taking your boat there. From St. Mandrier to Toulon the banks are lined with shipbuilding yards and industry with the exception of the small port of La Seyne. This, too, is surrounded by shipbuilding and St. Mandrier is much more congenial.

In these waters you must be on the look-out for naval manoeuvres and submarines. See The Pilot for Zones and Areas reserved for special purposes and practices such as submarine diving.

Toulon

Lat. 43° 7′ N
Long. 5° 56′ E

AVAILABLE: Water, fuel, repairs, hauling out, weather reports, all the facilities you would expect to find in a big dockyard town.

MOORINGS: Apply Capitainerie in centre of quay (Port du Commerce)

CHARGES: First three days free, then

	day	week	month	year
5 to 10 tons	5 F	30 F	105 F	900 F
10 to 20 tons	8 F	40 F	140 F	1,200 F

Coming up what has been called one of the finest roadsteads in the world you will see the dockyards and naval activities ahead

Toulon (*continued*) and, above them, the forts on the surrounding hills. Approaching, your course lies to the starboard side of all the harbour activity. The entrance to the yacht harbour is not at first very easy to distinguish against the background of flats with shops and pavement cafes on the promenade below them.

On entry between the red and green lights you will see yachts moored across to port but you should turn in to starboard to the yacht harbour.

The town, or at least, the port part of it is on the quay. You can drink at a pavement cafe and survey your boat over the wide promenade. The Musée Naval is here, housing splendid models of 18th century ships, paintings and figureheads plus interesting data about the history of French navigation.

Much damaged in WW2 Toulon is the principal naval arsenal of France and headquarters of the Mediterranean Fleet. Between the rebuilt port and the rebuilt town quite a number of the picturesque 18th century streets remain. Wandering from the yacht harbour to the town you can explore endlessly, finding new delights at almost every turn of a succession of narrow streets, small squares and alleyways.

Ste. Marie-Majeure Cathedral, part 13th century.
Fish Market 1549.
Hôpital Civil 1678 (founded).
Dolphin fountain 1782.
Flower Market in the rue d'Alger.
Daily market in the Cours Lafayette.

Toulon.

Harbours East of the Rhône 107

Hyeres

Lat. 43° 5' N
Long. 6° 10' E

AVAILABLE: Water, fuel, weather reports.
MOORINGS: Apply Capitainerie on nearest corner to you as you approach central projecting quay.
CHARGES:

	June—September		October—May	
	day	week	day	week
8 metres	7 F	35 F	7 F	18 F
10 metres	14 F	85 F	14 F	45 F

We always seem to enjoy our visits to Hyeres, the town of palm trees. The town is some distance from the yacht harbour but there are all shops near at hand.

Coming in through the narrow entrance you will see the moorings immediately to port or straight ahead; the Capitainerie at the end of the central projecting quay will direct.

Hyeres is a splendid clean harbour backed by palm trees and smart apartment blocks.

Although the town of Hyeres is two miles away inland it is well worth not one but many visits and there is a good bus service. The warmth, splendid air, palm tree-lined roads attracted many English people to live here after WW1; in fact it is regarded as being the oldest of what are known as the Riviera winter resorts.

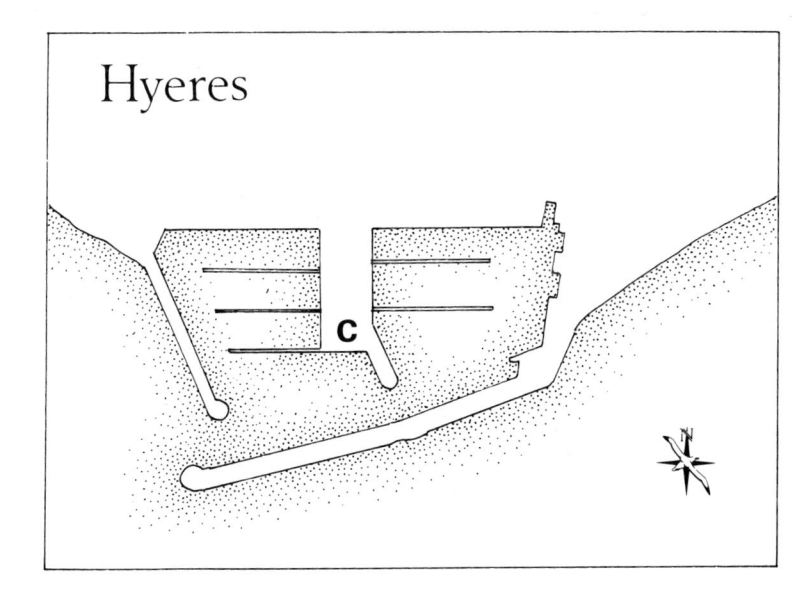

French Mediterranean Harbours

Hyeres There is a plaque on the wall of a house recalling that Robert
(continued) Louis Stevenson spent the happiest days of his life at Hyeres.
Whilst seeking improvement in his health here he wrote *Child's
Garden of Verses*, *Prince Otto* and *The Black Arrow*.

You get excellent vegetables here and earlier than anywhere
else. The displays in the market and in the narrow streets of the
old town are a delight.

Hyeres.

Porquerolles

Lat. 43° N
Long. 6° 12' E

AVAILABLE: Water.
MOORINGS: Apply Capitainerie at the shore end of the
mole.

Porquerolles

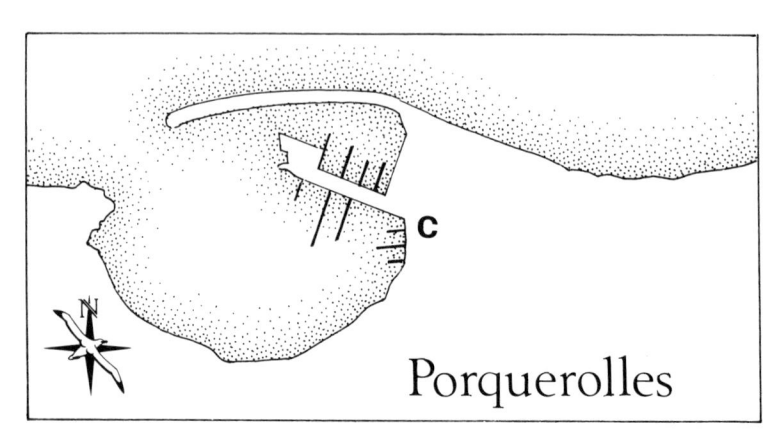

Harbours East of the Rhône

Porquerolles.

CHARGES:

	June—September		October—May	
	day	week	day	week
8 metres	7 F	35 F	7 F	18 F
10 metres	14 F	85 F	14 F	45 F

On entry proceed either side of the central mole from which leads the palm tree-lined quay to the shore and the Capitainerie.

From the moorings there are few buildings to be seen; the harbour area is quite a wide expanse bare of interest and the main road curves up from this to a small shopping area and a dignified and surprisingly large square.

Hotels, restaurants and shops all seem to have a rather old-fashioned air. There is no sign of any modern development which gives the place a quaint charm.

The island is unspoilt and beautiful. Cars are restricted. Some yachtsmen are happy to spend long periods here enjoying the beaches surrounded by lush vegetation, wild flowers and forests; others leave almost immediately complaining that there is nothing to do. If you are fond of walking you can visit the lighthouse, about three miles through the pine trees and heather to the south of the island.

Le Lavandou

Lat. $43° \, 30' \, N$
Long. $5°$ E

AVAILABLE: Water, fuel, weather reports, chandlery.
MOORINGS: Apply Capitainerie half-way along the quay to port on entry.

The hills that you see rising behind the town are the first of the Maures Mountains.

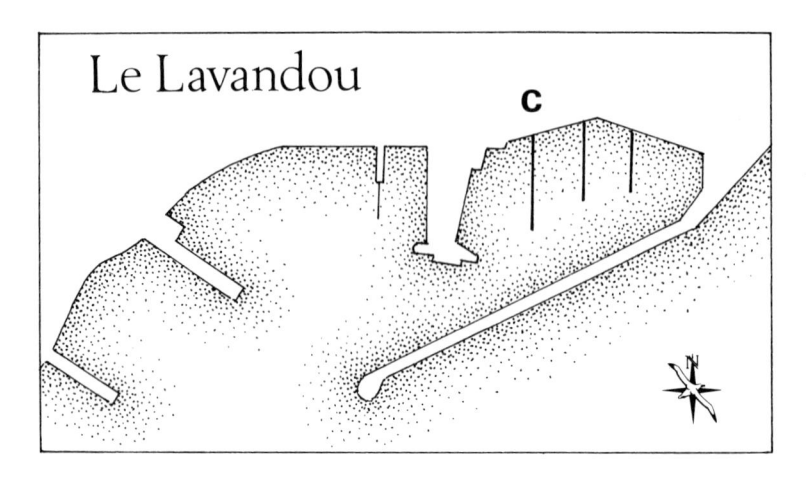

Le Lavandou

Le Lavandou, once a fishing village, is now a popular resort as it possesses a fine sandy beach which is one of its principal attractions.

There are a number of good chandlers' shops on the quay, a tree lined promenade with shops and cafes behind.

The moorings position is being improved but it is sometimes difficult to get in here.

Cavalaire-sur-Mer

Lat. 43° 10′ N
Long. 5° 32′ E

AVAILABLE: Water, fuel, weather reports.
MOORINGS: Apply Capitainerie on the quay near to the starboard jetty on entry.

Cavalaire.

Harbours East of the Rhône

As you approach it is interesting to reflect that this was the spot chosen for the landing of American and French forces thirty years ago (in August 1944). The extent and shelter of the beaches was the obvious reason for this choice.

The harbour of Cavalaire is small and the area around is bare and uninteresting. The town is a short walk away.

It is not a port that would appeal for a long stay despite the palm tree-lined beach.

St. Tropez

Lat. 43° 16′ N
Long. 6° 38′ E

AVAILABLE: Water, fuel, repairs, hauling out, weather reports.

MOORINGS: Apply Capitainerie on the inner quay facing you as you come in at the end to starboard.

You will see the citadel as you approach; rounding the mole the outer yacht harbour is then to starboard. The inner harbour ahead accommodates larger yachts and fishing boats and it is certainly most attractive with the Tour du Portaleb and the Tour Vielle as background extensions to the outer quay. Space is

St. Tropez.

St Tropez

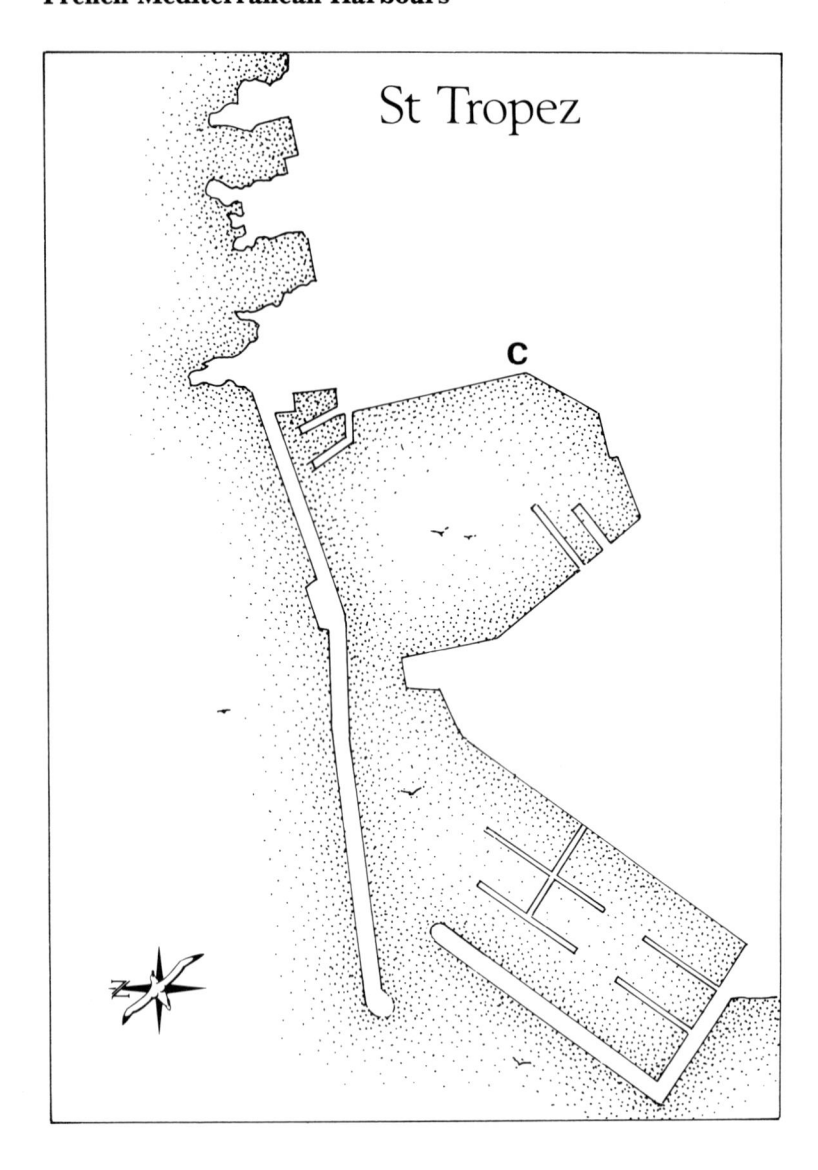

usually available on the long mole to port whilst enquiring about moorings.

There are all facilities around, quaint streets, quaint shops and it is a uniquely attractive place if becoming somewhat spoilt by its reputation. It has been the meeting place and temporary home of artists and writers for years but since publicised in the press as

Harbours East of the Rhône

the haunt of film stars you can just imagine the sophisticated environment. Around the fringe of the inner harbour, where the big luxury yachts lie stern to, life throbs with With It people of all ages; you may simply love this of course.

The citadel, referred to earlier, is a part 16th century fortress, at present a naval museum.

Musée de l'Anonciade, by the quay, houses a splendid collection of modern art.

See The Pilot for details of Firing Practice areas and procedure in the Golfe de St. Tropez.

Port des Marines de Cogolin

Lat. $43°\ 16'\ N$
Long. $6°\ 35'\ E$

AVAILABLE: Water, fuel, repairs, hauling out, weather reports, electricity.
MOORINGS: Apply Capitainerie, in harbour at head of quay to port.

Advertised as the roomiest, best equipped and cheapest port on

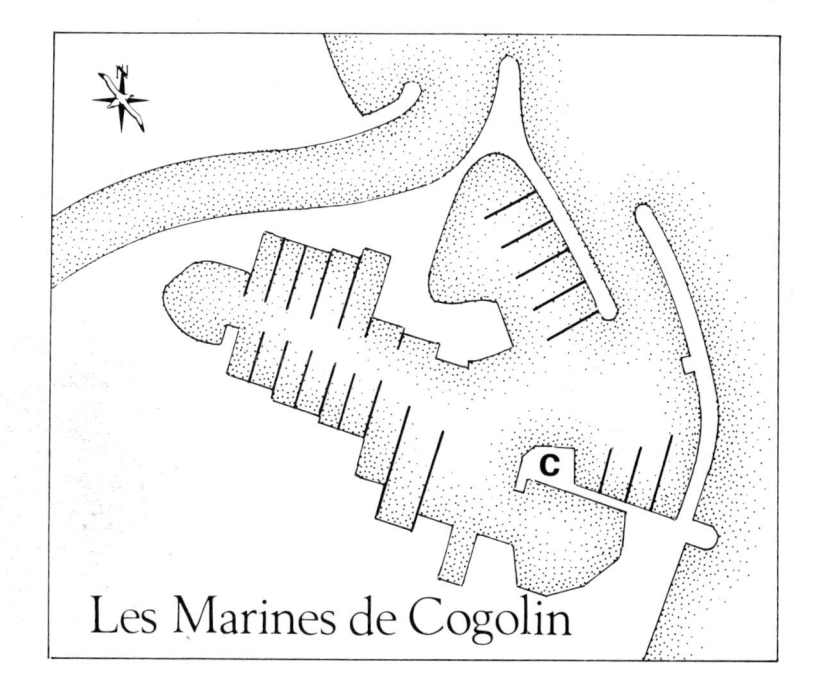

Les Marines de Cogolin

Port de Cogolin (*continued*) the Côte d'Azur, Port de Cogolin is able to accommodate 1,500 boats in its 76 acres of harbour, with a depth of over 3 m.

Around the three basins are the light ochre and beige-pink houses that go with the moorings, all new and all part of the complex built by Sofirev and financed by Rothschild.

There are new shops along the new quays, a Post Office, bank, chemist, bookshop, fashion, furniture, car-hire, restaurants; a night-club where you dance in three inches of sea-water (barefoot, of course, not in your half-boots), a large screen cinema, a bridge club.

The berths in the basins are bought on a semi-permanent basis; you buy so many shares in the Port Company according to the size of your boat.

Outside of the basins is what is known as the Open Harbour for short staying boats; this means you and me. There is nothing here within walking distance outside of the harbour and you may find the outer harbour of nearby St. Tropez more convenient.

(See map on page 113.)

Port Grimaud.

Port Grimaud

Lat. 43° 17′ N
Long. 6° 36′ E

AVAILABLE: Water, fuel, weather reports.
MOORINGS: Apply Capitainerie to starboard at harbour entrance.

A very small harbour in this newly created and fashionable model fishing village with waterway 'streets' of sophisticated houses leading off, like a modern miniature Venice. It is only a short sail across, and further in to, the bay from St. Tropez.

On entry there will appear to be a confusing selection of waterways available but you will see the Capitainerie to starboard. You may also see other yachts sailing other ways; they will be residents sailing home up their 'street' securing at the bottom of their garden. Over the tops of houses you see sails moving.

It is all most unusual. A novelty to see perhaps but more like a stage set than a cruising man's harbour and therefore hardly a serious consideration for a stay when Ste. Maxime and St. Raphael are within view.

Shops are available.

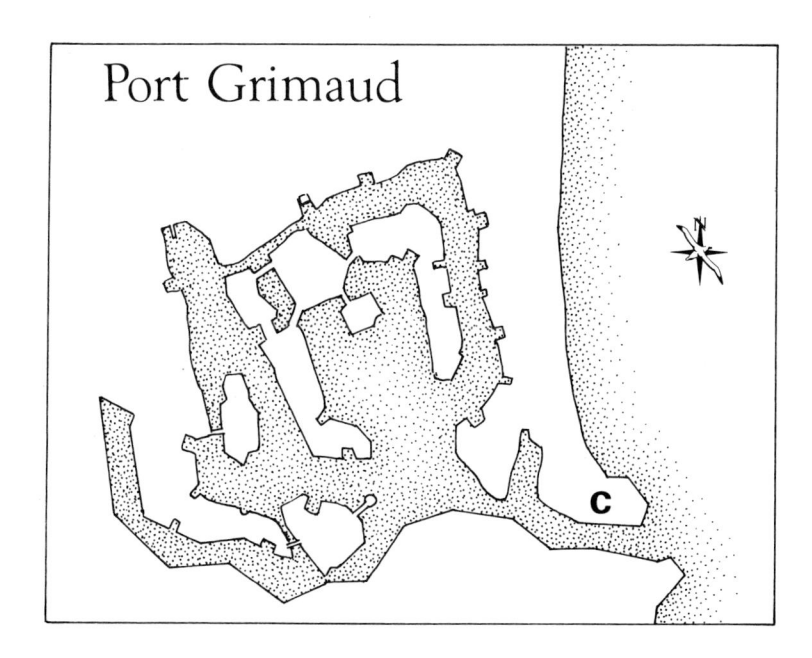

Ste. Maxime

Lat. 43° 18′ N
Long. 6° 38′ E

AVAILABLE: Water, fuel, repairs, weather reports, chandlery, electricity.

MOORINGS: Apply Capitainerie on the central mole.

CHARGES:

	June—September			July/August month	October—May		
	day	week	month		day	week	month
8 m	12.60 F	64.80 F	252 F	336 F	8.40 F	25.20 F	100.80 F
10 m	18.00 F	90.00 F	342 F	456 F	12.00 F	36.00 F	144.00 F
12 m	22.50 F	112.50 F	414 F	552 F	14.40 F	43.20 F	174.00 F
14 m	31.50 F	157.50 F	558 F	744 F	19.20 F	57.60 F	240.00 F

Across the gulf from St. Tropez the fashionable resort of Ste. Maxime has a splendid harbour, larger than it looks at first sight,

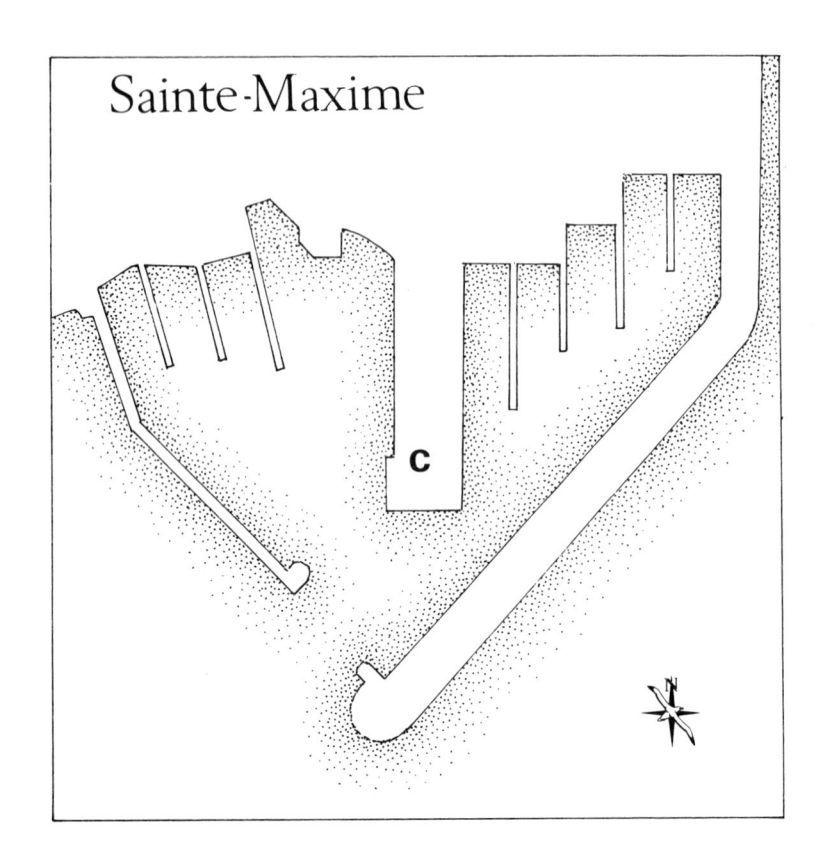

Ste. Maxime.

facing south and well sheltered.

There are all facilities and all shops around the harbour for the town is within easy wandering distance of your boat. You step ashore to the Place du 15 Août 1944 which is the day Ste. Maxime was liberated. It is a very pleasant place indeed, a family seaside town, ideal for a long stay.

Mooring charges for a year at Ste. Maxime
8 metre	1,488 F
10 metre	2,160 F
12 metre	2,760 F
14 metre	3,720 F

St. Raphael

Lat. 43° 25′ N
Long. 6° 48′ E

St. Raphael.

St. Raphael AVAILABLE: Water, fuel, repairs, weather reports, chandlery,
(*continued*)   electricity.
             MOORINGS: Apply Capitainerie on the quay, starboard side,
                          at the far end of the harbour (looking from the
                          entrance).
             CHARGES:

First day free, then:

	October — May			June and September		
	day	week	month	day	week	month
8 metre	4.50 F	27 F	99 F	15 F	100 F	385 F
10 metre	9 F	55 F	187 F	20 F	132 F	484 F
12 metre	11 F	77 F	253 F	27 F	176 F	660 F
14 metre	13 F	88 F	352 F	30 F	198 F	726 F

	July			August		
	day	week	month	day	week	month
8 metre	16 F	110 F	418 F	18 F	121 F	468 F
10 metre	22 F	143 F	540 F	24 F	160 F	605 F
12 metre	29 F	187 F	715 F	30 F	198 F	726 F
14 metre	31 F	209 F	770 F	32 F	220 F	803 F

Coming in to the Golfe de Fréjus you will see the new Port Saint Raphael to starboard. The old port lies further on ahead but it is mainly used by fishing and pleasure boats and small boats, crowded in on the limited pontoons; such facilities as exist there are rather primitive and why should they be otherwise when a brand new yacht harbour (for which you pay), lies a short distance away?

An impressive feature of sailing this coast is the striking contrast of the blue sea against the red rocks. St. Raphael is very pleasantly situated.

On entry in to the yacht harbour you do not see the Capitainerie immediately because it is situated right down at the other end. The yachting facilities are splendid with one of the best selections of chandlery to be found anywhere; also shops of yachting interest, provisions and a bar-cafe.

St. Raphael is within view all round the bay. From the yacht harbour it is quite a walk to the town, a good deal of the way on splendid beaches. It is a health resort for the treatment of rheumatism, in fact it was a health resort in Roman times. The

Saint-Raphael

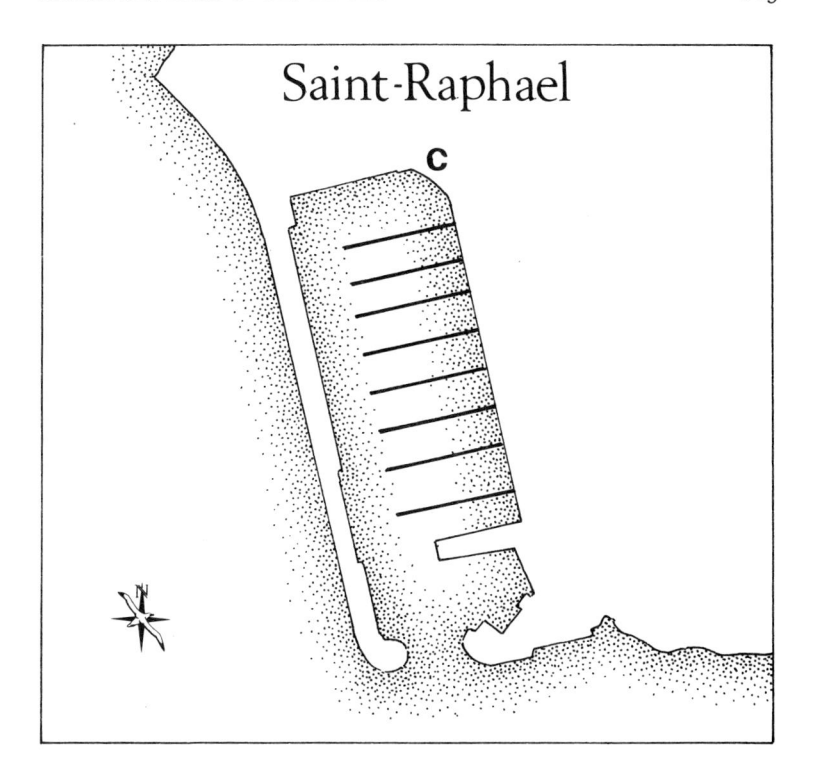

c

summers are moderate and the winters mild.

The monument just behind the old harbour recalls that the victorious Napoleon landed here on his return from Egypt in 1799. Fifteen years later the defeated Napoleon left St. Raphael for Elba.

Mooring charges for a year at St. Raphael
8 metre	2,200 F
10 metre	3,100 F
12 metre	3,900 F
14 metre	4,600 F

French Mediterranean Harbours

Port du Trayas

Lat. 43° 29′ N
Long. 6° 56′ E

AVAILABLE: Water, fuel, weather reports, electricity.
MOORINGS: Apply Capitainerie at the back of the white building on the quay.
CHARGES:

	June—September			October—May		
--	day	week	month	day	week	month
6 to 9 metres	25 F	150 F	600 F	12 F	75 F	300 F
9 to 13 metres	40 F	240 F	950 F	20 F	120 F	450 F
13 to 20 metres	70 F	420 F	1600 F	35 F	210 F	800 F

Surrounded by a background of wooded hills this is a very pretty little port.

It is all very new. The toilet and shower block—the Capitainerie is at the back of the same building—would not disgrace a first-class hotel.

There is a restaurant and bar actually on the quay with an immaculate private beach just beyond.

Notices are written in French and English so that obviously English speaking visitors are expected. But when you see the size of the car park in relation to the port and learn that there is one car parking place for each yacht berth you realise that this is a car owner's harbour; without a car you would find Port du Trayas most inconvenient for there are no shops near.

Port la Galere

Lat. 43° 30′ N
Long. 6° 57′ E

AVAILABLE: Water, fuel, weather reports.
MOORINGS: Apply Capitainerie on the further projecting quay.

A small harbour. Although classed as 'private' (and, indeed, it is very private), visiting yachts are welcome and it is therefore included.

Although the width of the harbour entry is given as 50 yards the approach is positively hair-raising, coming in with the steep rocks close to starboard. In anything but settled weather it should not be attempted without local knowledge.

There is room for nearly 200 boats; maximum LOA 12 metres.

(Map and continuation on page 122.)

Harbours East of the Rhône

Port la Galere.

French Mediterranean Harbours

A new supermarket is conveniently situated on the quay.

The port has been created with, and principally for, the houses of the port, a new marine paradise, 'the most original and successful architectural triumph around the entire Mediterranean basin'. If you are interested in architecture you should come in here and wander round ashore. Every line and angle that could be possibly considered as ordinary or commonplace has been rigorously excluded. The point of this marine paradise is that people are supposed to buy apartments or villas here and you could get a nice little flat for around £50,000.

It is interesting but not intended to cater for yachting gypsies like you and me. Without a car you cannot get anywhere ashore outside of this paradise.

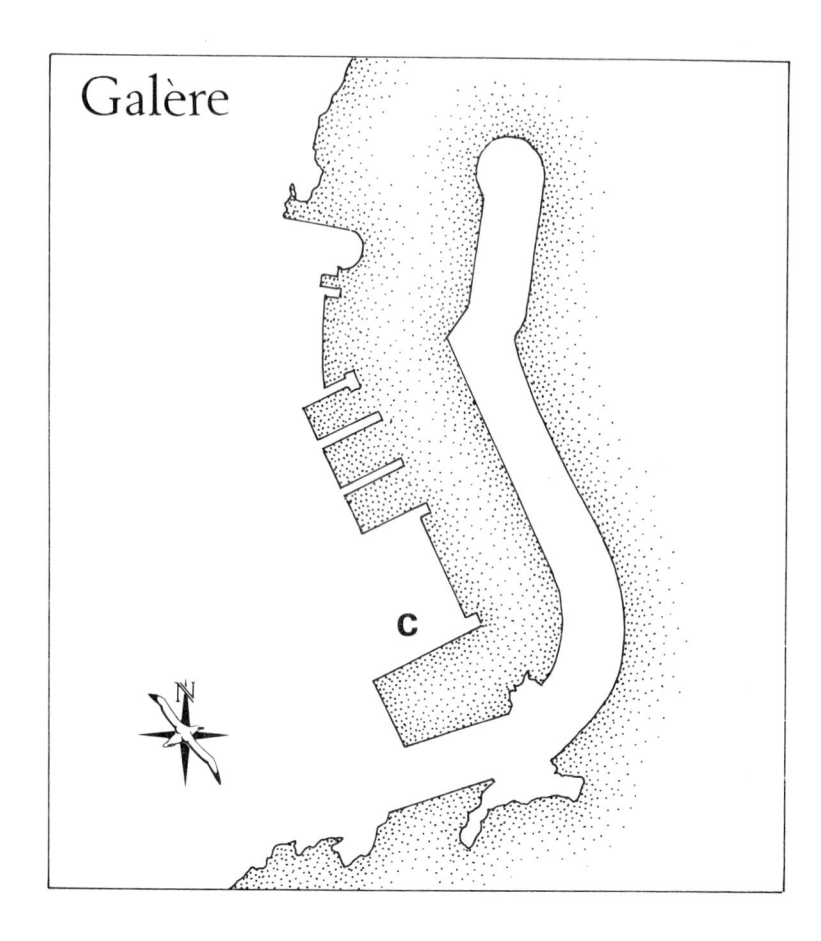

Galère

Theoule sur Mer

Lat. $43° 51' N$
Long. $6° 57' E$

AVAILABLE: Water, fuel, weather reports.
MOORINGS: Apply Capitainerie, on the quay ahead just beyond the central pontoon.

A very small harbour tucked in under the Theoule promontory, fairly full with the fishing boats and resident boats that occupy the deep water berths near the entrance; further in there is less than 1 metre. It is not easy to find a berth here but the splendid alternatives of Port de la Rague and Port Mandelieu—La Napoule are within view.

Theoule-sur-Mer.

French Mediterranean Harbours

Port de la Rague

Lat. $43° 31' N$
Long. $6° 57' E$

AVAILABLE: Water, fuel, hauling out, weather reports, chandlery, electricity.

MOORINGS: Apply Capitainerie, at the far end of the harbour to port.

CHARGES:

	October—May			June—September		
	day	week	month	day	week	month
10 metres	7.20 F		180 F	14.40 F	90 F	384 F

In the Golfe de Napoule now there is an embarrassment of moorings from which to choose (needed in the season of course); you will not be in any doubt having established the position, but positive identification is confirmed when you get near by the

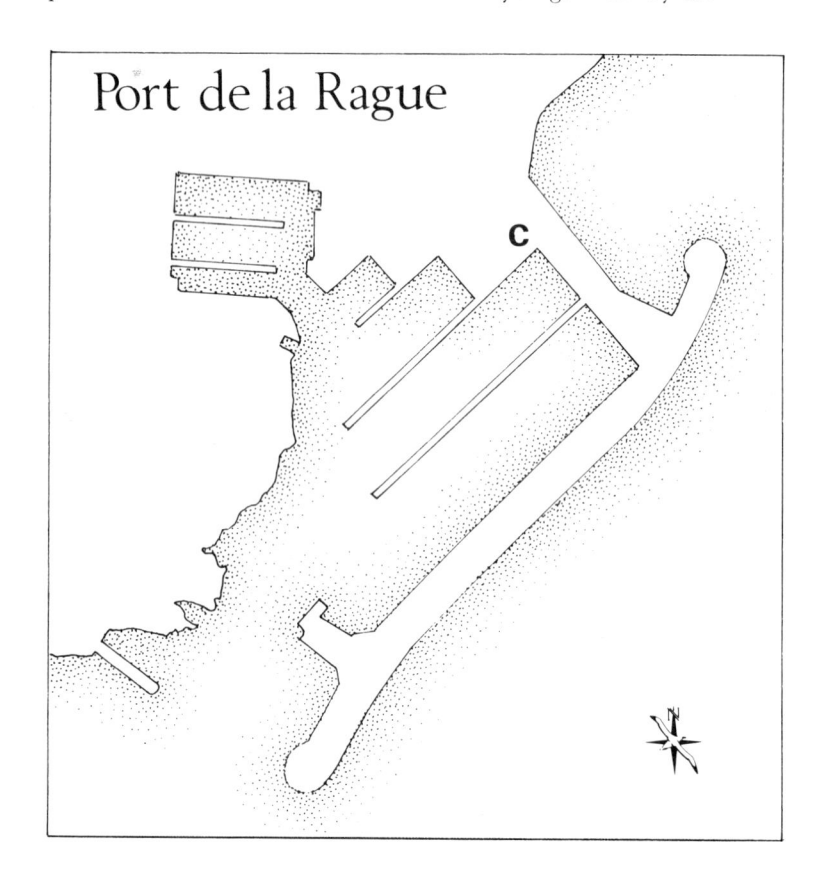

Port de la Rague.

white beacon with a green band bearing the name 'PORT DE LA RAGUE'.
This is a big harbour and there are big yachts here. All services for your boat are available including good chandlers' shops, also wintering facilities afloat or ashore.
There are no ordinary shopping facilities however although it is said that shops are planned for the harbour area. Outside there are no shops, no village, just a lonely main road. The visiting yacht needs to come in here well provisioned.

Port de Mandelieu—La Napoule

Lat. 43° 32′ N
Long. 6° 56′ E

AVAILABLE: Water, fuel, repairs, weather reports, chandlery, electricity.

MOORINGS: Apply Capitainerie in the mushroom building to port on entry.

CHARGES:

	June—September			October—May		
	day	week	month	day	week	month
8 metre	15 F	75 F	300 F	10 F	50 F	200 F
12 metre	30 F	150 F	600 F	18 F	90 F	360 F
18 metre	45 F	225 F	900 F	24 F	120 F	480 F

Mooring charges for a year

8 metre	2,400 F
12 metre	4,320 F
18 metre	5,760 F

French Mediterranean Harbours

Mandelieu la Napoule

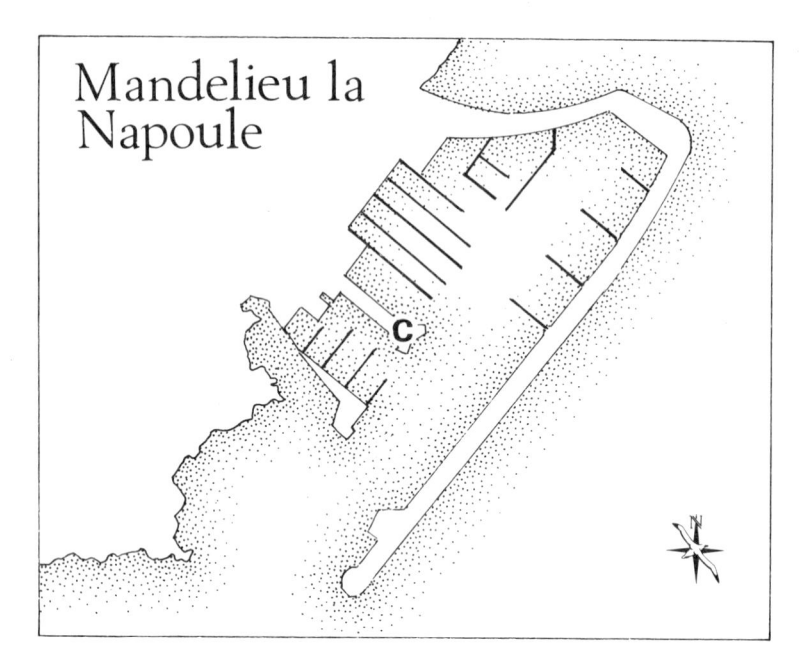

Three miles from Cannes. The beacon at the entrance is inscribed on a large white band with the name of the port.

This is an enormous harbour with room for nearly 1,500 boats. There are all facilities including wintering afloat or ashore, a most impressive line of shops on the quay, food, tobacco, chandlers, agencies of marine equipment, brokers, cafes, even a laundrette (any female member of your crew will confirm that this alone is worth coming in for). Should there be any mutinous members of your crew there is a travel agency.

Outside of the harbour area there is nothing of interest in the immediate vicinity.

Mandelieu—La Napoule.

Cannes

Lat. $43° 33'$ N
Long. $7° 1'$ E

AVAILABLE: Water, fuel, repairs, hauling out, weather reports.

MOORINGS: Apply Bureau du Port, near root of starboard quay.

CHARGES:

	June—September			October—May		
	day	week	month	day	week	month
5 to 10 tons	9 F	55 F	195 F	2 F	13 F	37 F
10 to 15 tons	11 F	70 F	250 F	2.50 F	16 F	47 F
15 to 20 tons	14 F	90 F	310 F	3 F	20 F	55 F
20 to 50 tons	21 F	140 F	490 F	7 F	45 F	140 F

You will expect this harbour to be crowded for the fabulous reputation of Cannes is fully justified. Do not let this deter you from coming in however; do be prepared for the swell as you round the end of the outer mole, also to meet traffic coming out which will be leaving the black topped circular marker to port as you will be.

Once in the harbour you have to turn slightly to starboard, down past the millionaire's row of yachts. Even if surveyed by

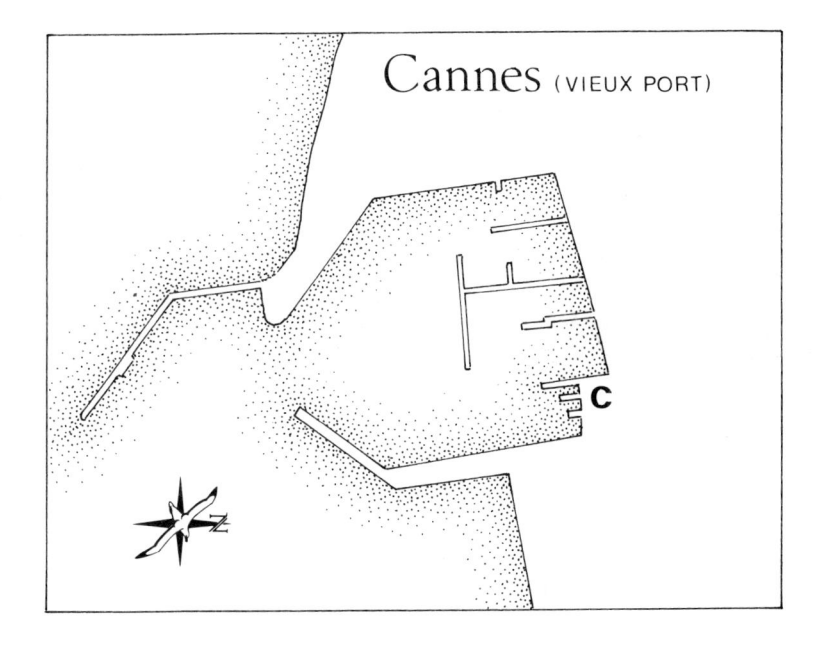

French Mediterranean Harbours

bikini beauties or professional crews, take your time, do it all slowly. It is likely that you will be seen and directed, for it is a most efficient harbour, contact between quays and the bureau du port being maintained by short wave radio. There are facilities for wintering afloat and ashore.

The beach is on the other side of the main quay, backed by palm trees, gardens, beautiful wide streets, flower beds, the flower market, every shop that you could wish for.

The main jetty is named Jetée Albert-Edouard in honour of Edward VII of England, a frequent visitor to Cannes when Prince of Wales.

Cannes.

Cannes—Port Pierre Canto

Lat. 43° 32′ N
Long. 7° 2′ E

AVAILABLE: Water, fuel, repairs, weather reports, chandlery, electricity.

MOORINGS: Apply Bureau du Port, on quay to starboard.

CHARGES:

	June—September day	week	October—May day	month
5 to 20 tons	17 F	111 F	6 F	180 F
20 to 50 tons	25 F	168 F	11 F	325 F

At the other end of the bay from Port de Cannes, this is a large, gleaming new harbour with an avenue of shops in the port area, splendid quays, flowers all round and big car parks.

The quay shops include a chandlery, nautical instrument servicing, chemist, bank and restaurants.

To moor your beautiful yacht here would be an inexpensive way (comparatively), of living on the front of the most aristocratic of the Côte d'Azur resorts; this may have occurred to the owners of some of the resident yachts who competed for the berths when they first became available.

But the cruising yachtsman wanting to stroll ashore will find only a suburb of splendid apartments surrounding the harbour. Port Pierre Canto is too far from the centre of Cannes to be of

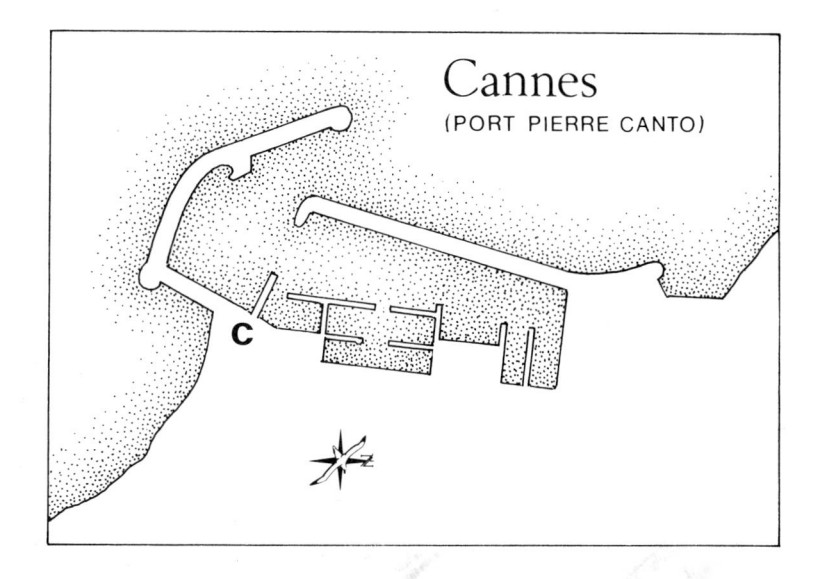

Cannes
(PORT PIERRE CANTO)

Port Pierre Canto in the Bay of Cannes.

interest to the yachtsman without shore transport.

On approaching Port Pierre Canto you will see another harbour to starboard; this is Port Palm Beach for small boats only.

Within Port Pierre Canto.

Harbours East of the Rhône 131

Golfe-Juan

Lat. 43° 34′ N
Long. 7° 5′ E

AVAILABLE: Water, fuel, repairs, hauling out, weather reports, chandlery.
MOORINGS: Apply Capitainerie on quay to port on entry.
CHARGES: Free for first three days.

A very pleasant, smallish harbour, ideal for craft up to around ten metres. All facilities are here.

Golfe-Juan.

Golfe-Juan
(continued)

The shops and town are alongside the harbour, within strolling distance of your boat. It is a gay little town, rather more homely and less expensive than its neighbours.

When Napoleon returned from Elba on the 1st March 1815 he landed here.

Port Gallice—Antibes

Lat. $43° 34' N$
Long. $7° 7' E$

AVAILABLE: Water, fuel, weather reports, chandlery, electricity.
MOORINGS: Apply Capitainerie, on shore quay at further end from entrance.
CHARGES:

	October—May			June—September		
	day	week	month	day	week	month
10 metres	12 F	90 F	360 F	27 F	200 F	810 F

Although so described, Port Gallice is not at Antibes but about ten miles away. It is a private harbour, very large and full of all sorts of yachts up to the millionaire class. Naturally there are all facilities here. There are some shops in the harbour area but the surroundings are residential.

The harbour is pleasant enough but there are much gayer surroundings just around the corner at Port Vauban.

Port Gallice.

**Port Gallice-
Antibes**
(*continued*)

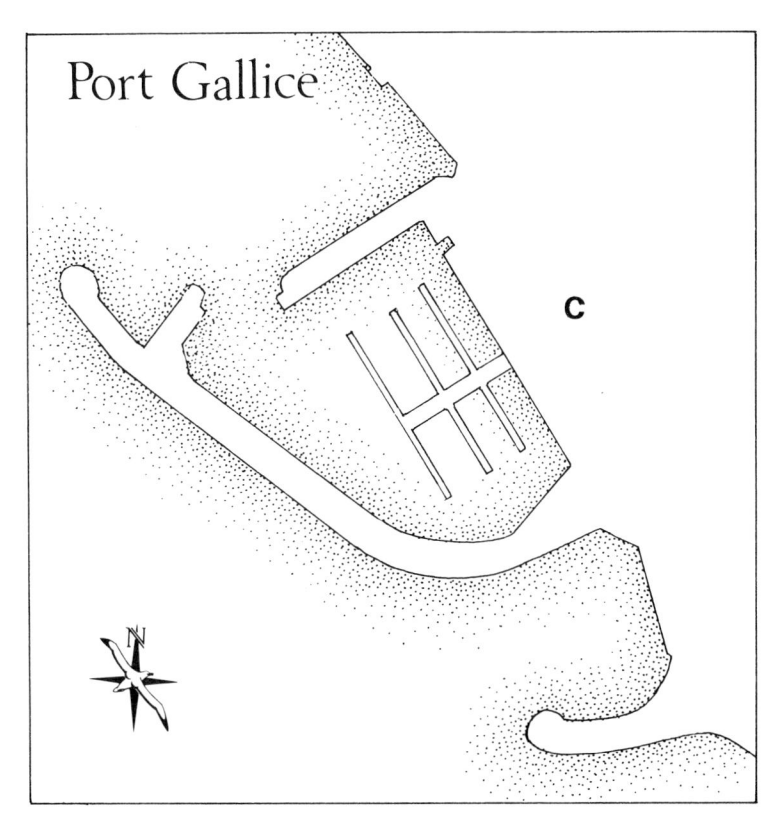

Port Gallice

Port Vauban—Antibes

*Lat. 43° 35′ N
Long. 7° 8′ E*

AVAILABLE: Water, fuel, repairs, hauling out, weather reports, chandlery, electricity.
MOORINGS: Apply Capitainerie, to port after passing jetty to port.
CHARGES:

	June—September		*October—May*	
	day	*week*	*day*	*week*
6 metres	11 F	75 F	3 F	18 F
8 metres	15 F	80 F	3 F	18 F
10 metres	19 F	110 F	6 F	33 F
15 metres	29 F	160 F	13 F	75 F

Every time we come in here it seems to get bigger—there must

French Mediterranean Harbours

Port Vauban

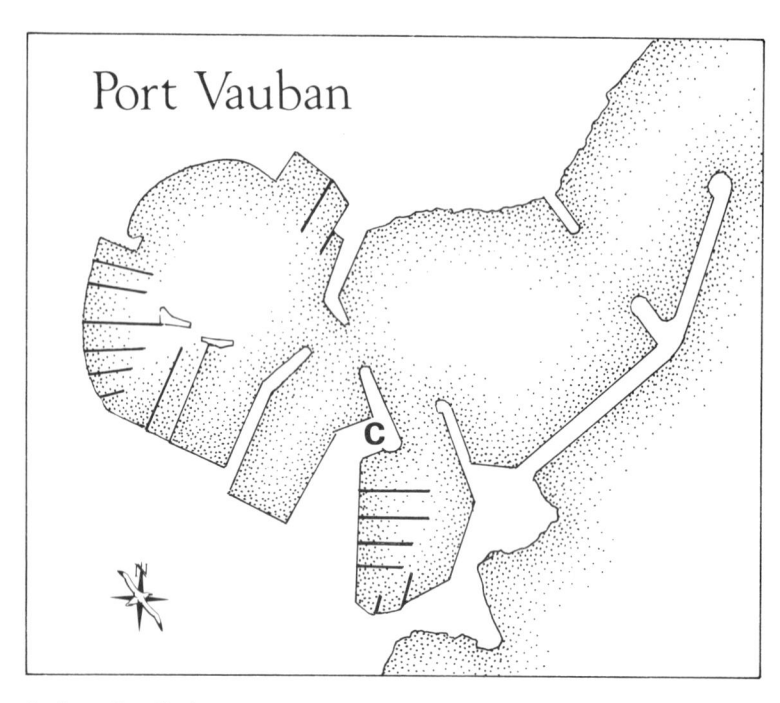

Antibes—Port Vauban.

Harbours East of the Rhône

be acres of boats in this fascinating harbour. Many cruising yachtsmen get settled in here for a long time. If anything needs doing to your boat this is undoubtedly the place to do it. It is the ideal harbour in many ways, with everything for your boat and a great deal of interest for you; an old town, shops, bars right by the quayside.

In the Château Grimaldi there is a wonderful Picasso collection.

Baie des Anges — Port de Marina

Lat. $43° 40' N$
Long. $7° 13' E$

AVAILABLE: Water, fuel, weather reports, electricity.
MOORINGS: Apply Capitainerie, to port on entry.
CHARGES:

	October — May			June & September			July & August		
	day	week	month	day	week	month	day	week	month
8 m	5 F	30 F	110 F	16 F	100 F	380 F	18 F	120 F	450 F
10 m	9 F	65 F	240 F	20 F	120 F	450 F	23 F	140 F	550 F
12 m	12 F	75 F	280 F	28 F	180 F	700 F	30 F	190 F	720 F
15 m	17 F	110 F	420 F	34 F	235 F	900 F	37 F	250 F	950 F

Baie des Anges.

French Mediterranean Harbours

Baie des Anges

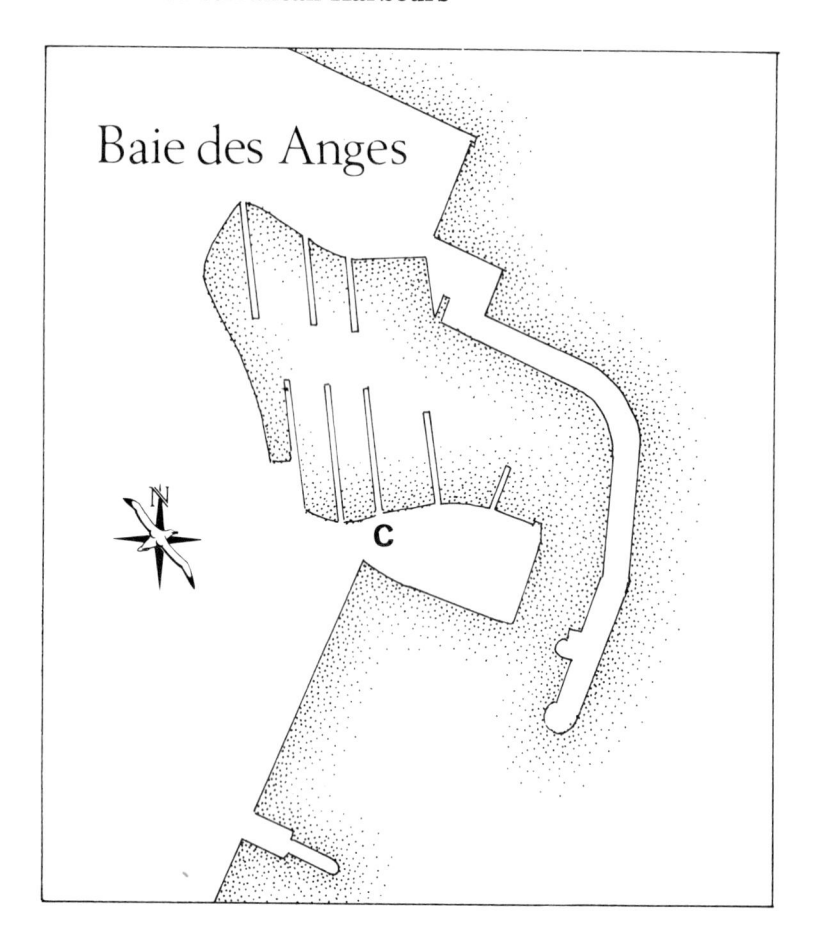

An excellent new harbour with apartment blocks of such striking design that they seem to flow above you. They, of course, are the reason for the existence of the port, all part of this fantastic residence-cum-yacht park complex.

There are some interesting shops already in the harbour area and there will be more, enough, possibly to 'keep you in at nights' which would be just as well because outside there is nothing but traffic tearing in and out of Nice.

Harbours East of the Rhône

Nice

Lat. $43° 42' N$
Long. $7° 17' E$

AVAILABLE: Water, repairs, chandlery.
MOORINGS: Apply Capitainerie, past third jetty to starboard, on entry corner of main harbour to starboard.

Your eyes may have difficulty in picking out the entrance to the harbour against the background of buildings and mountains; your ears will be in no doubt about the proximity of Nice for the crescent of surrounding hills encloses and concentrates the roar of the big jet planes as they struggle up into the blue sky from Nice Airport.

To starboard immediately on entry, and to seaward of the steamer quay, you will see a small yacht harbour but you proceed on past this when the main yacht moorings will be seen to starboard.

Nice—the ferry steamers now have been moved to the outer harbour.
Photo: French Government Toursit Office.

Nice

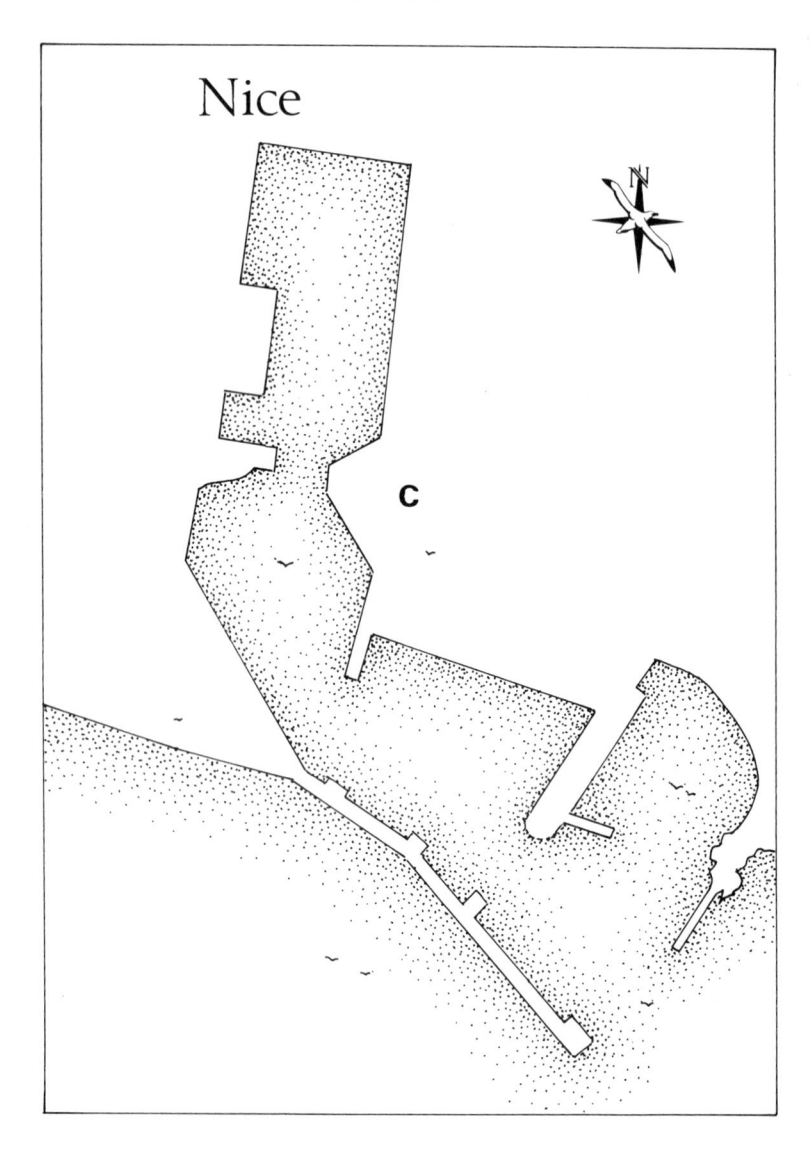

On the quay road behind them are vast chandlery displays and yachting facilities. As you might expect there is everything you need here.

Nice is principally a commercial harbour with commercial quays and environment, but there are plans to extend the yachting facilities. The ferry steamer berths have been moved to the outer harbour.

Nice.

There is a great deal of life and bustle all around, the old part of the town is a warp's length away and you are enclosed on three sides by traffic.

Along from the harbour is the three mile sea front and Promenade des Anglais, backed by hotels and apartments of émigrés from all over the world; behind are glittering shops, department stores, cafes, neon lights, a cosmopolitan and exciting atmosphere.

Villefranche

Lat. 43° 42′ N
Long. 7° 19′ E

AVAILABLE: Water, fuel, repairs, hauling out, weather reports.

MOORINGS: Apply Capitainerie, at inner end of harbour by drydock.

CHARGES:

	June—September			October—May		
	day	week	month	day	week	month
5 to 10 tons	7.50 F	45 F	150 F	1.50 F	9 F	30 F
10 to 15 tons	10 F	60 F	200 F	2 F	12 F	40 F
15 to 20 tons	12.50 F	75 F	250 F	2.50 F	15 F	50 F

140   **French Mediterranean Harbours**

Villefranche

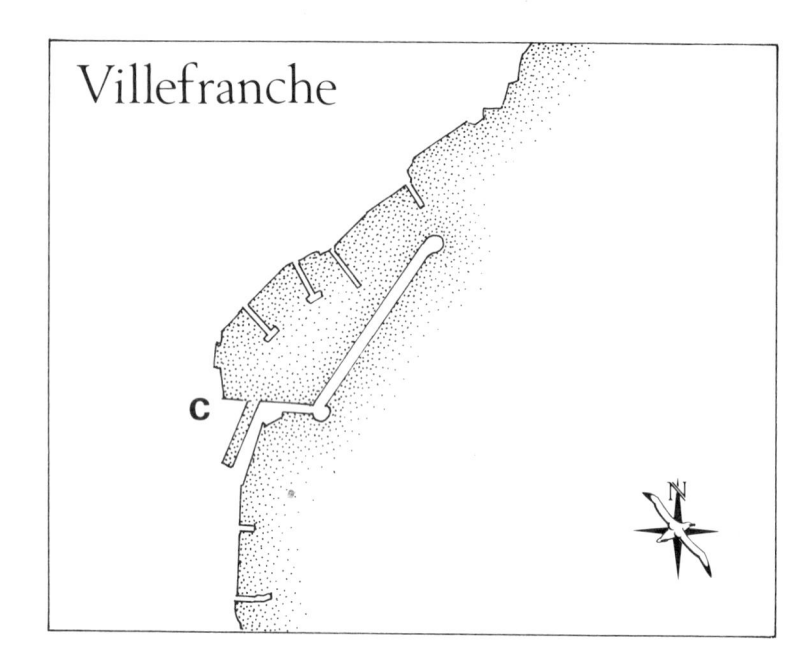

Villefranche is a favourite harbour of ours.

Harbours East of the Rhône

A favourite harbour of ours, perhaps popular with us because it does not seem to have changed, at least not in the last ten years; perhaps because of the beauty of the bay in which this well sheltered harbour is situated.

The attractions here include good old fashioned yacht yard facilities including a drydock that can handle craft up to about 200ft LOA.

It is a pleasant walk from the harbour up into the delightfully unspoilt town. Modern development seems to have passed Villefranche by and it is the better place for it.

It is, of course, a naval station and you often see warships anchored in the bay.

Villefranche—a pleasant walk from the harbour up into the unspoilt town.

St. Jean-Cap-Ferrat

Lat. 43° 41′ N
Long. 7° 20′ E

AVAILABLE: Water, fuel, weather reports, electricity.
MOORINGS: Apply Capitainerie, on the inner harbour quay ahead.
CHARGES:

	October—May			June—September		
	day	week	month	day	week	month
Port public 10 metres	4.50 F		105 F	16.50 F		99 F
	plus T.V.A., water, electricity etc.					
Port privé	12 F inclusive.		300 F	22.50 F	150 F	600 F

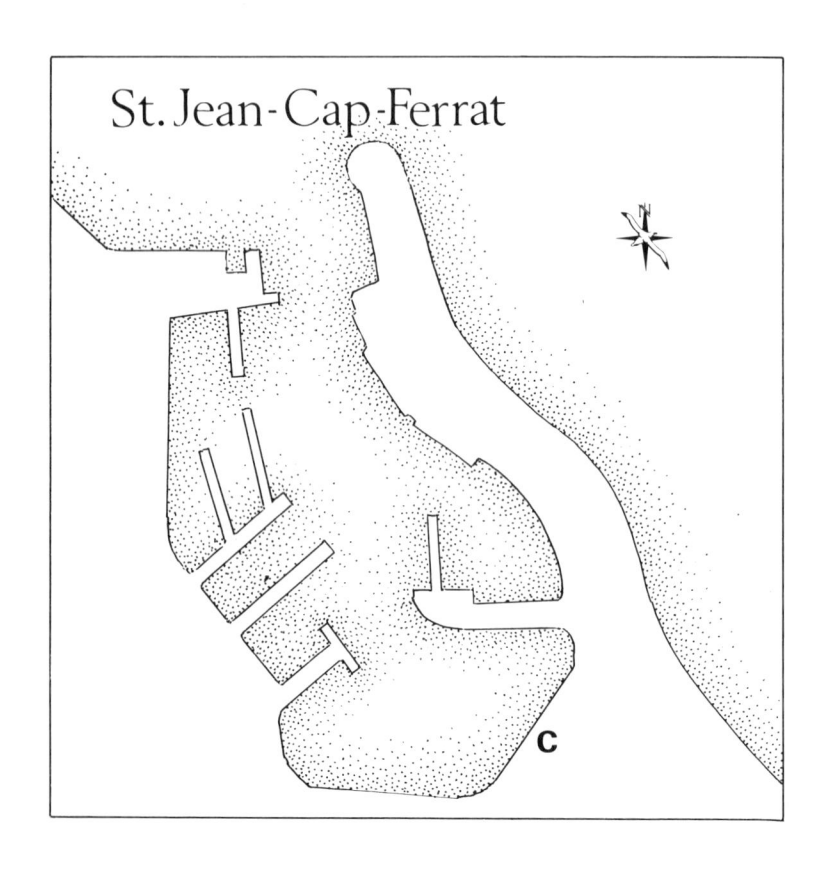

Harbours East of the Rhône

St. Jean-Cap-Ferrat is a personal little harbour.

This harbour has been enlarged and now accommodates big luxury yachts on the outer mole. The enlargement has not spoilt its character, however, but has added up to date yachting facilities.

If you can get into a nice berth you will not want to leave; it is so pleasant and uncrowded ashore with the villas of the wealthy all around. It seems to be such a personal little harbour that you come to regard it as your own.

Pleasant shops are within view and only a pleasant stroll away.

French Mediterranean Harbours

Beaulieu-sur-Mer

Lat. 43° 43′ N
Long. 7° 20′ E

AVAILABLE: Water, fuel, repairs, hauling out, weather reports, chandlery, electricity.

MOORINGS: Apply Capitainerie, at root of central projecting mole.

CHARGES:

	June—September			October—May		
	day	week	month	day	week	month
5 to 20 tons	19 F	120 F	460 F	6 F	35 F	145 F
20 to 50 tons	30 F	200 F	700 F	13 F	80 F	315 F

There are two harbours at Beaulieu; the first is small with depths of less than 1 metre. The second, the main yacht harbour, is distinguished by the outer mole guarding the entrance. You leave this mole or breakwater to port on entry and then turn in to starboard to this really fabulous yacht harbour, set amidst rich green vegetation, flowers and palm trees all around.

There is a selection of shops in the harbour area supplying food, bread, books, stationery, clothes, laundry facilities, jewelry, also a chemist and a selection of restaurants.

The fashionable winter resort of Beaulieu is near.

Beaulieu.

Beaulieu-Sur-Mer

Monaco

Lat. $43° 44'$ N
Long. $7° 26'$ E

AVAILABLE: Water, fuel, repairs, weather reports, chandlery, electricity.
MOORINGS: Apply Harbour Master, starboard quay on entry.
CHARGES: 1 F per gross ton covers a period of ten days.

As you approach the unmistakable Port de Monaco you will see a new harbour being created on your port side; this is the new Port de Fontvieille with apartment blocks around, the design

Monaco is quite unmistakable.

Monaco

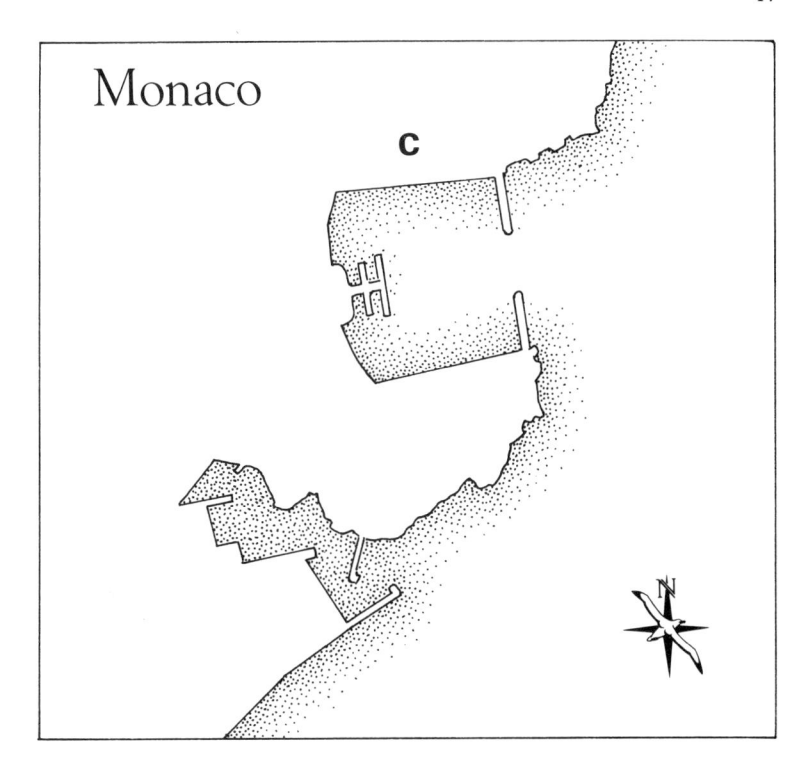

c

of which resembles the opening petals of a flower.

With the reputation that Monaco enjoys it will be obvious that it will not always be possible to find a berth here. But there is plenty of room in the harbour for manoeuvring and there needs

The entrance to Monaco Harbour.

Monaco
(*continued*)

to be when you get yachts in here which could (and do), carry on their decks craft superior to the humble sloop that is our pride and joy.

The Monaco Guide Book says 'there is no place on earth where one can find per square metre so many occasions for having fun, relaxing and enriching one's cultural outlook'. Those of us who find many occasions for examining our dwindling supply of money can still wander happily on the fringe of all this luxury.

The Guide goes on to say 'passing yachts are in a position, without any prior formality whatever, to connect themselves with the water supply, electricity supply and the networks of international telephones and television'. There cannot be many grander harbours in the world.

Monaco (population 1,700), is the old capital up on the rock, La Condamine (11,500), is the area round the harbour and Monte Carlo (10,000), is slightly to the north-east.

You should see the Museum of Oceanography which is open all the year. The Prince's Palace is open from July to September. Another date to bear in mind is the end of May/beginning of June when the Monaco Grand Prix is held.

Berths may be hard to find in Monaco, but there is plenty of room for manoeuvring.

Port Communal—Menton

Lat. $43° 47' N$
Long. $7° 31' E$

AVAILABLE: Water, fuel, weather reports, chandlery, electricity.
MOORINGS: Apply Capitainerie, at the shore end of the harbour.

An adequate harbour that gets rather crowded with smaller boats despite the fact that there is something of a swell in here at times.

The area surrounding the quay is rather dusty and unkempt; what few shops there are, and the surrounding buildings, look like the poor relation of the smart Port Garavan within view across the bay.

Although nearer to the town it is not so pleasant a harbour as Port Garavan. Both have the same climate, of course, which is one of the mildest on the Riviera. Menton is sheltered by mountains from the mistral and is one of the most popular winter resorts in France.

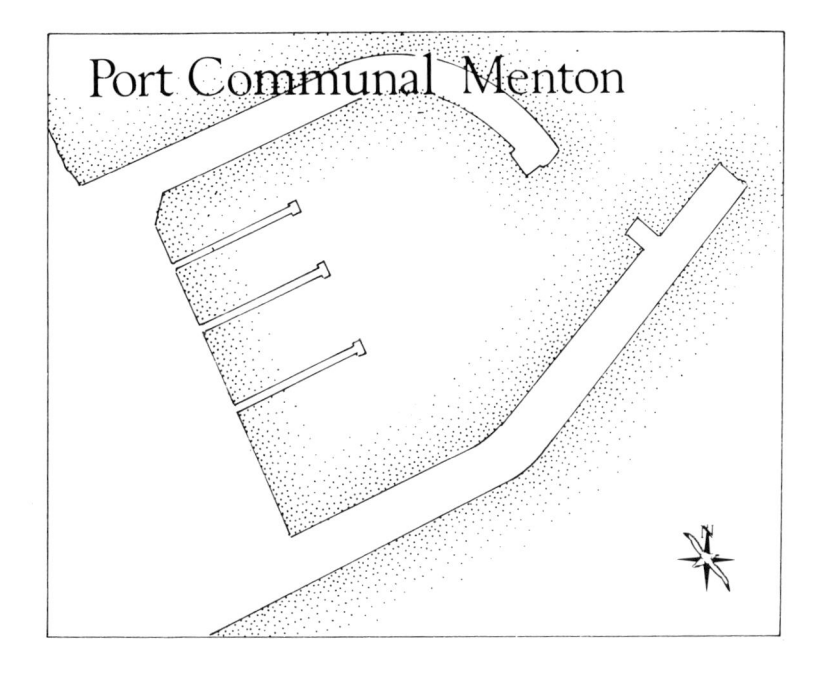

Port Garavan—Menton

Lat. 43° 47′ N
Long. 7° 31′ E

AVAILABLE: Water, fuel, repairs, weather reports, chandlery, electricity.
MOORINGS: Apply Capitainerie, at harbour entrance.
CHARGES:

	October—May			June—September		
	day	week	month	day	week	month
10 metres LOA	11.90 F	75.70 F	263.20 F	24.50 F	159.70 F	550 F

The last port on the French Mediterranean coast and only a five minute cruise away from Italy. Port Garavan is an excellent large harbour suitable for all sizes of yachts up to the largest and we have always received efficient attention here.

In bad weather the approach can be a bit hair-raising for you seem to be coming right on to the beach before making your turn in to port and the breakers are somewhat intimidating.

Surrounding the harbour are gracious villas in an avenue lined

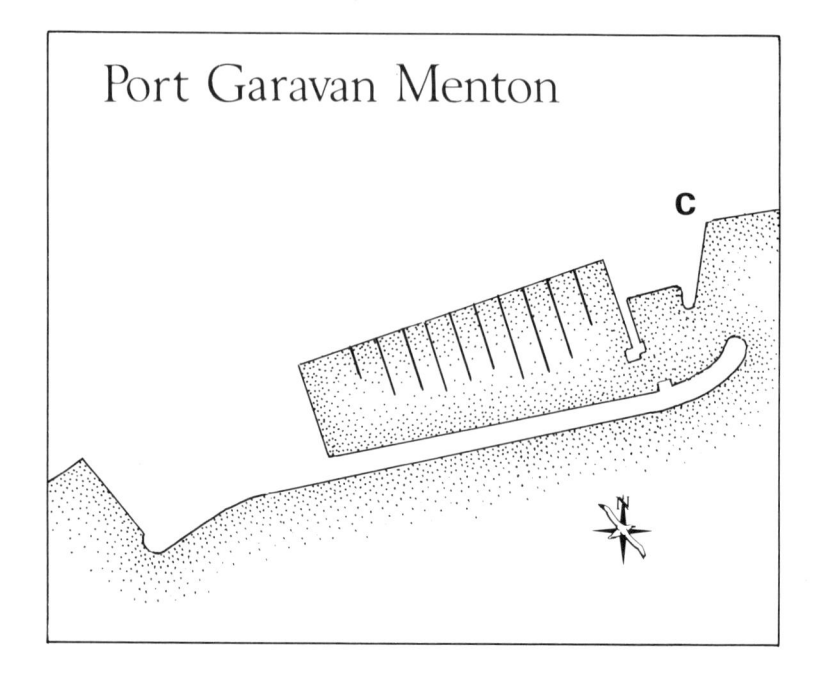

Harbours East of the Rhône

Port Garavan is an excellent large harbour for yachts.

with palm trees and spectacular cliffs look right down into the cockpit.

There are shops around, including a big new supermarket adjacent to the yacht harbour.

The charming town of Menton is within view.

8 Corsica

Distances between harbours

Calvi to	Kms
Girolata	32
Porto	14
Cargesse	33
Sagone	11
Ajaccio	46
Porto Pollo	37
Propriano	11
Bonifacio	64
Porto-Vecchio	53
Pinarello	22
Bastia	125
Macinaggio	32
Centuri	30
Saint-Florent	32
Ile-Rousse	41
Calvi	23

Distances to Corsica
from NICE to
Calvi	180
Ile-Rousse	182
Ajaccio	240
Bastia	230

from MARSEILLE to
Calvi	310
Propriano	320
Bastia	390

from TOULON to
Ile-Rousse	260
Ajaccio	260

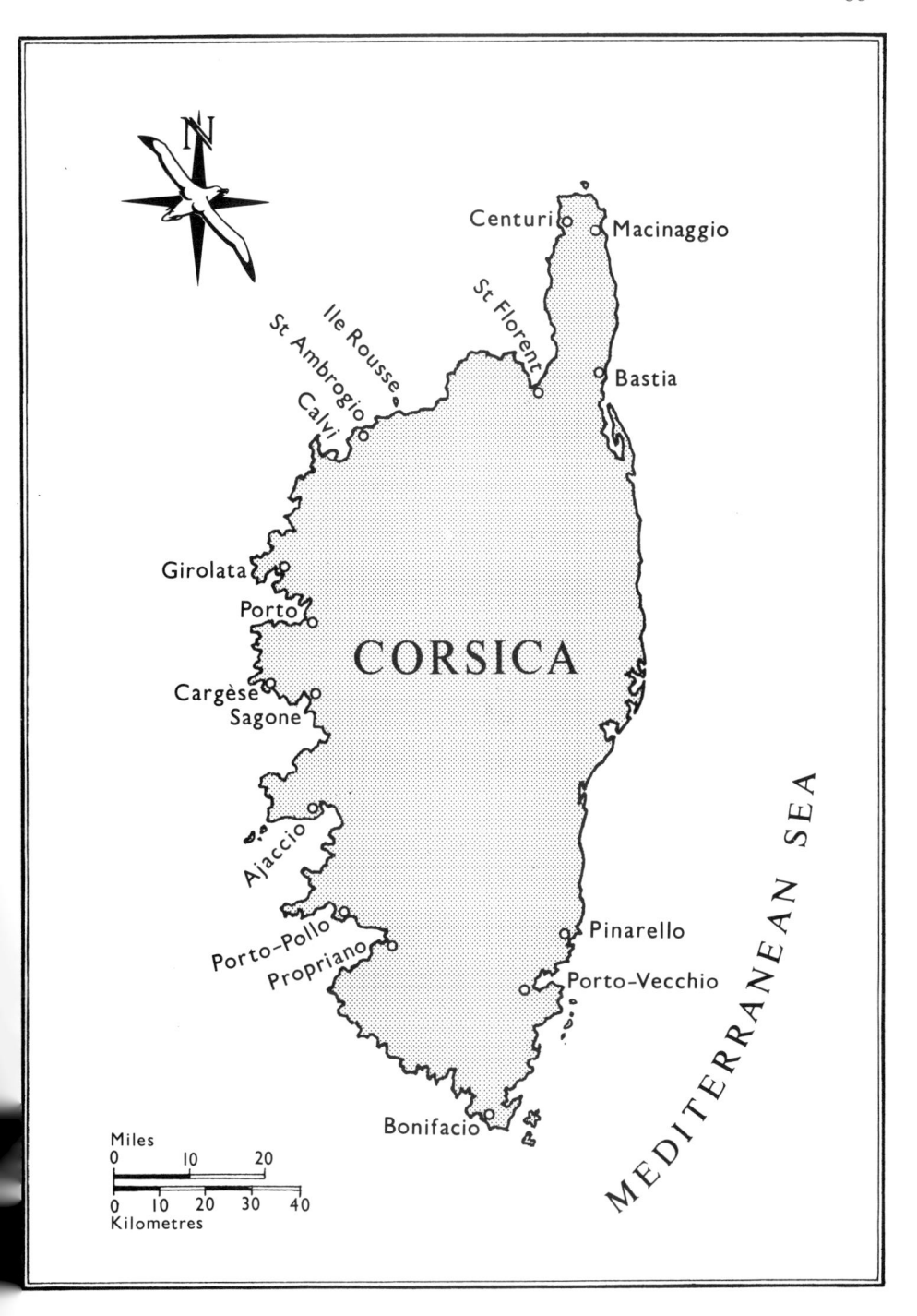

CORSICA

Calvi (Corsica)

Lat. $43° 34'$ N
Long. $8° 46'$ E

AVAILABLE: Water, fuel, weather reports.
MOORINGS: Apply Capitainerie on quay.

Nearest to France and one of the most attractive harbours in the island, Calvi is well sheltered. On rounding the mole you will see yachts moored stern-to on the quay ahead; you should not secure to the quay immediately to starboard on entry for this is the ferry steamer berth.

Above the harbour towers the Genoese citadel. Around are pavement cafes under the palm trees; all shops are in the delightful small town only a short walk away and there is a market.

The whole of the bay is fringed with a sandy beach, backed

Reproduced from British Admiralty Chart No. 1126 with the sanction of the Controller H.M. Stationery Office, and of the Hydrographer of the Navy.

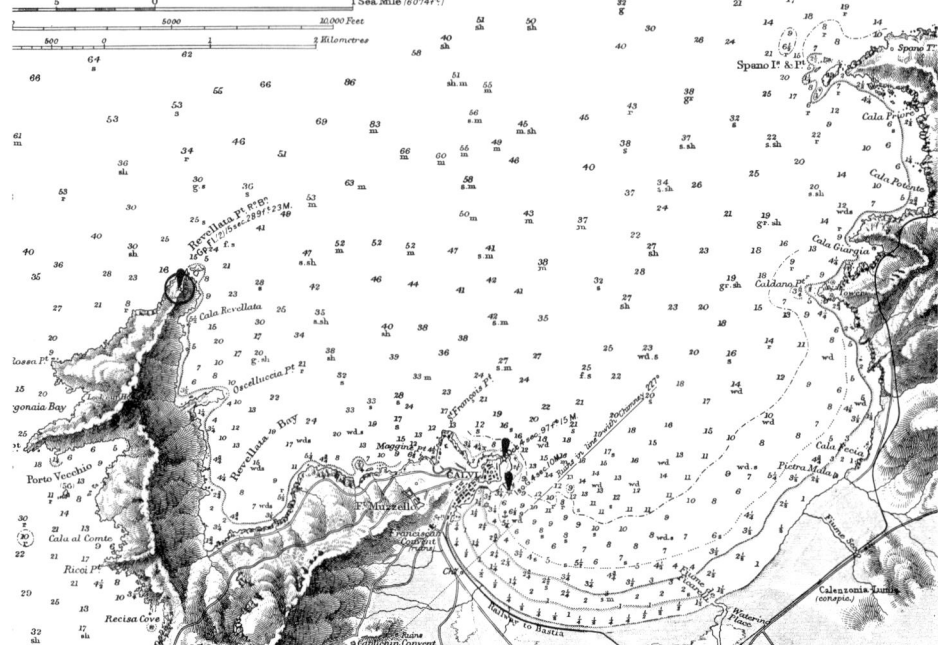

Corsica

One of the most attractive harbours in Corsica . . .

and shaded by pine trees. Calvi is a most delightful place, the sort of place where the weeks pass and you say you must get on but are most reluctant to do so. Many others feel the same way of course and a cosmopolitan yachting crowd fills the harbour in July and August.

Christopher Columbus was born in Calvi.

. . . Calvi is well sheltered.

French Mediterranean Harbours

Girolata (Corsica)

Lat. 42° 21′ N
Long. 8° 37′ E

AVAILABLE: Nothing.

An anchorage that you should only explore in settled weather and not when the wind is in the SW. In a beautiful setting against a background of mountains, Girolata is completely isolated.

Porto (Corsica)

Lat. 42° 16′ N
Long. 8° 42′ E

AVAILABLE: Nothing alongside.

The red rocks and green valley provide a beautiful setting but this is an anchorage only. Even in the slightest swell you would have an uncomfortable job getting a dinghy alongside the small quay.

Once ashore it is very pleasant. Around the quay are restaurants but there are other shops in the village, a short and pretty walk up the road.

Porto.

Cargesse (Corsica)

Lat. 42° 8′ N
Long. 8° 36′ E

AVAILABLE: Nothing.

Simply an open anchorage, not recommended if the wind is in the SW and a long way away from the village.

A beautiful situation and a beautiful sandy beach upon which to pull up the dinghy.

Sagone (Corsica)

Lat. 42° 7′ N
Long. 8° 42′ E

AVAILABLE: Nothing.

A beautiful bay with beaches all round and backed by mountains. Coming into the bay you will see a small quay across to port but it really is small and most yachts anchor off.

There is not much point in coming ashore to this quay with the thought of getting provisions for there is nothing here; the few shops are right over on the other side of the bay.

There can be an uncomfortable motion here particularly with the wind in the south; but in the customary good weather this is a beautiful place in which to find peace and seclusion.

Sagone Bay has beaches all round, backed by mountains.

French Mediterranean Harbours

Ajaccio (Corsica)
Lat. $41° 56' N$
Long. $8° 45' E$

AVAILABLE: Water, fuel, repairs, hauling out, weather reports, chandlery.

MOORINGS: Apply Capitainerie, between yacht harbour and steamer quay.

Capital of Corsica, birthplace of Napoleon (15th August 1769). As you come in to the Bay of Ajaccio you may notice a harbour across to starboard on the opposite side of the bay; this belongs to the naval authorities. To port is the town and you will see three harbours. Turn in round the first jetty although you may notice other yachts ahead and beyond the steamer quays.

Ajaccio
Reproduced from British Admiralty Chart No. 1126 with the sanction of the Controller H.M. Stationery Office, and of the Hydrographer of the Navy.

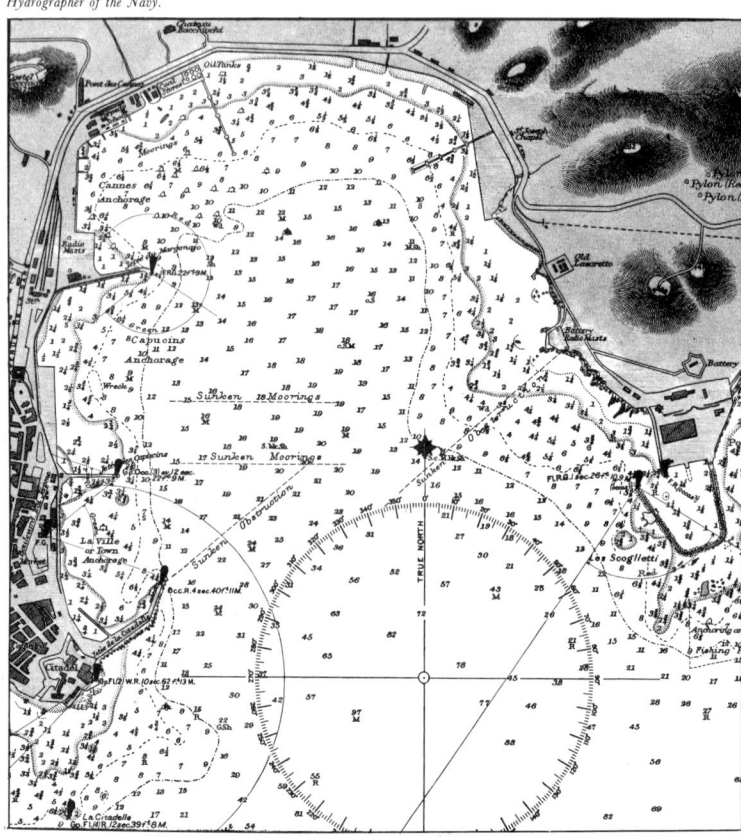

Corsica

Ajaccio has excellent facilities.

There are all facilities here in good old-fashioned boatyard style; in fact after the impeccable smartness of the Côte d'Azur marinas it is somehow satisfying to see some honest boating junk on the quay, bits of old tore-outs, rusty anchors and engine parts. But do not be put off by this homely idiosyncrasy of mine; Ajaccio is a splendid place in every respect with all facilities available.

There are good shops, spacious squares, wide avenues, picturesque alleyways in the town, a short walk up the palm tree-lined avenue from the quay.

Napoleon's birthplace is open to visitors. There is the Musée Napoléonien in the Town Hall.

Musée Fesch (Cardinal Fesch was related to Napoleon), houses the best collection of Italian paintings in France outside the Louvre.

Porto-Pollo (Corsica)

Lat. 41° 42′ N
Long. 8° 48′ E

AVAILABLE: Nothing.

An anchorage in a sandy bay, fringed with rocks and the usual splendid beach. If you are interested in skin diving you would like it here. There is little of interest ashore except the scenery and a few houses and hotels.

Porto Pollo Anchorage
Reproduced from British Admiralty Chart No. 1126 with the sanction of the Controller H.M. Stationery Office, and of the Hydrographer of the Navy.

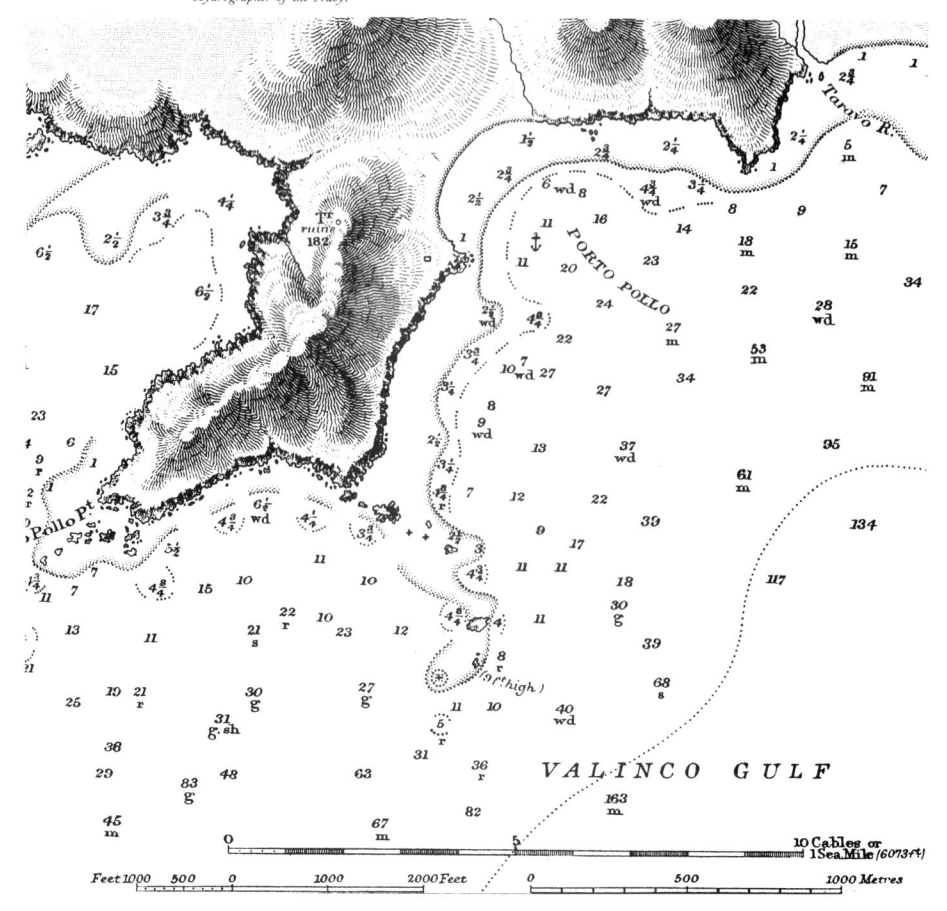

Propriano (Corsica)

Lat. 41° 41′ N
Long. 9° 16′ E

AVAILABLE: Water, fuel, weather reports.
MOORINGS: Apply Capitainerie on the shoreside quay.

As you approach Propriano appears to be a delightful small port in an attractive mountain background but on closer inspection the buildings around do not seem to be worthy of this setting. However, the harbour area and water front is gay enough.

Keep clear of the commercial quay used by the ferry steamers; you will see the stern-to yacht moorings. There is quite a swell in here when the wind is in the west but the actual harbour is pleasant enough and there are shops and some facilities.

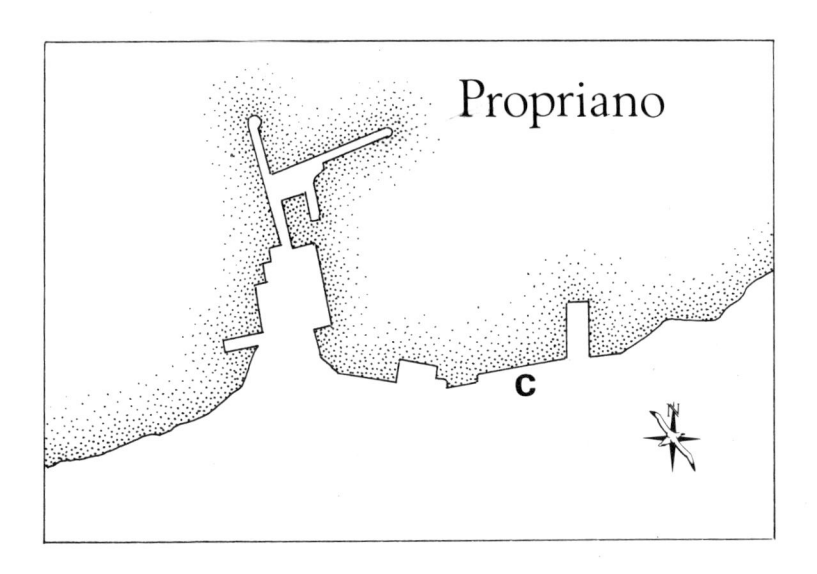

Bonifacio (Corsica)

Lat. $41° 23' N$
Long. $9° 9' E$

AVAILABLE: Water, fuel, repairs, hauling out, weather reports.
MOORINGS: Apply Capitainerie, to starboard half-way between Catena inlet and inward end of harbour.

A magnificent natural harbour dominated and overlooked by the 13th century Genoese fortress city. The limestone promontory

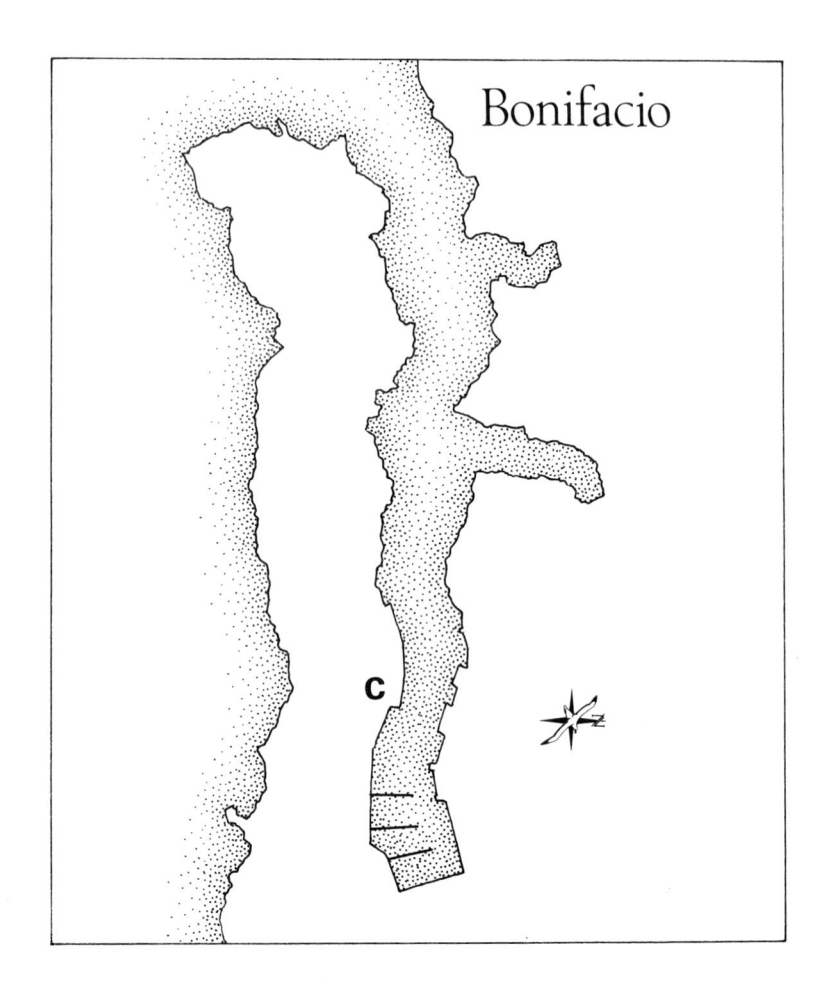

Corsica

on which Bonifacio is built runs parallel to the mainland and the creek between is the harbour. It is a strange medieval place.

As you enter you see the huge arc that has been weathered out of the rock. As you proceed up the inlet you look up apprehensively at the fortifications that seem to be in danger of falling over the precipitous sides.

Advancing into the inlet—half-way up to port you will see yachts up the Catena creek but this is the Chantier Navale—you should carry on to the end where you will see the stern-to yacht moorings by the yacht club.

Le Port Prive is planned to materialise here with accommodation for 1,200 yachts.

There are all facilities. Bonifacio is a strange town with massive

The entrance to Bonifacio Harbour with the west coast of Corsica behind.

Bonifacio
(*continued*)

Massive ramparts rise above Bonifacio Harbour.

walls and ramparts, a pleasant harbour area with hotels and restaurants around.

In less than an hour you can sail to Sardinia from here.

Across the Strait of Bonifacio can be seen the mountains of Sardinia behind the Isle of Lavezzi.

Corsica

Porto-Vecchio (Corsica)

Lat. $41° 35'$ N
Long. $9° 18'$ E

AVAILABLE: Water, fuel, weather reports, chandlery.
MOORINGS: Apply Capitainerie, at end of shoreside quay furthest from mole.

At the top of a sheltered bay five miles long by two miles wide and surrounded by impressive mountain scenery, Porto Vecchio is an old fortified town that has been rather neglected.

Proceed to the end of the harbour where you will see yachts moored. This is a commercial and fishing boat harbour and there is sometimes room on the commercial quay.

There are shops in the town but it is quite a walk away. It is not really a very inspiring place for a cruising yacht but there are plans for improving it.

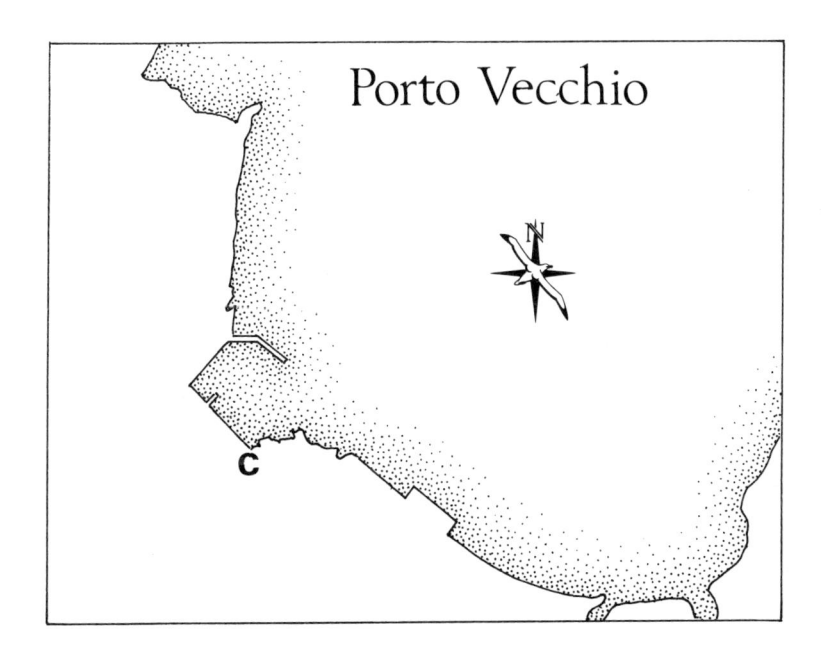

# Bastia (Corsica)

Lat. 42° 42′ N
Long. 9° 27′ E

AVAILABLE: Water, fuel, repairs, weather reports, chandlery.
MOORINGS: Apply Capitainerie at end of commercial quay.

Bastia, largest city in Corsica, is a fascinating place and in the yacht harbour you are right in the middle of it.
Approaching Bastia it will be apparent that the commercial

Reproduced from British Admiralty Chart No. 1126 with the sanction of the Controller H.M. Stationery Office, and of the Hydrographer of the Navy.

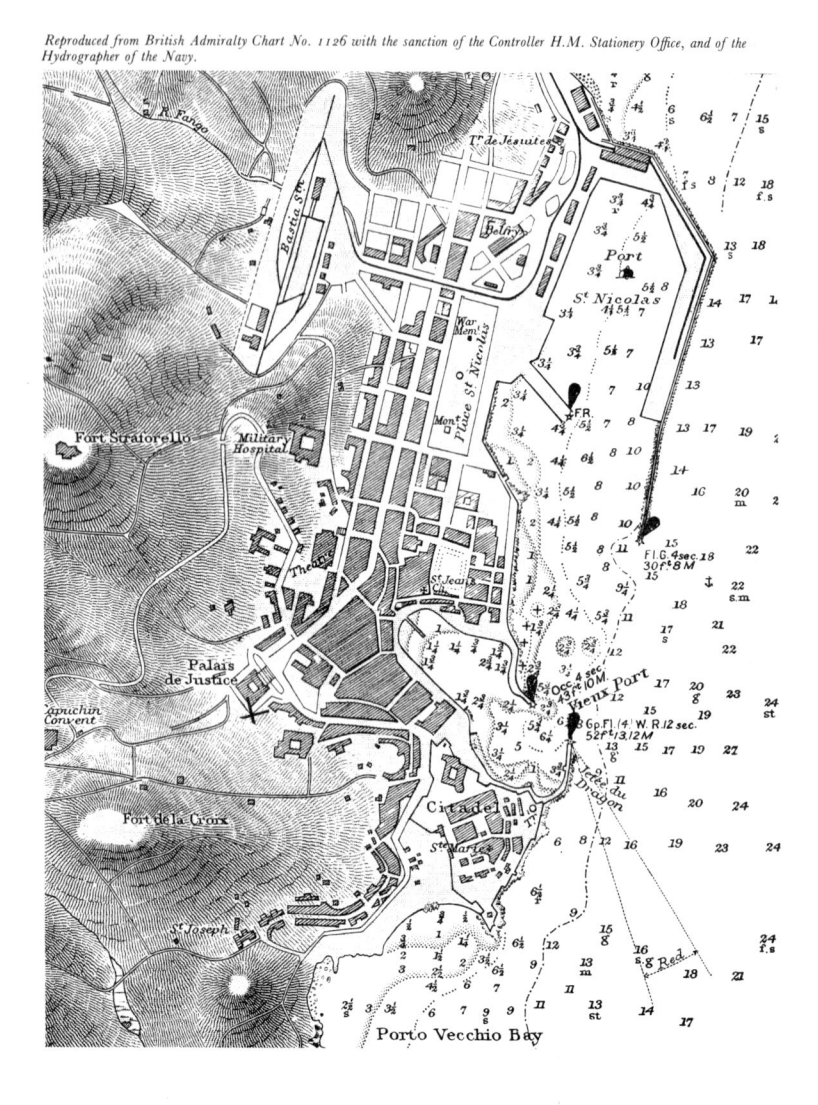

Corsica

Bastia, largest city in Corsica, has a yacht harbour in its centre.

harbour is to starboard of the yacht harbour for there is usually a ferry steamer or two in port and sometimes a large yacht keeping them company.

On entering the yacht harbour you will first see yachts anchored in the centre but it is more convenient to secure stern-to on the quay immediately to starboard.

Around part of the yacht harbour and in the streets leading up from it are skyscraper tenement blocks, basically drab and old yet colourful with displays of washing and seeming to hum with vitality. At the height of summer it is like being in a lively oven.

Pavement cafes add colour and all the shops you need are close by in the town.

You will either love or hate the bustle and life and noise of Bastia.

168   **French Mediterranean Harbours**

Macinaggio (Corsica)

Lat. 42° 57′ N
Long. 9° 27′ E

AVAILABLE: Water.

A pretty little place but very small indeed and not suitable for the average sized cruising yacht as most of the harbour is shallow, and most certainly not if the weather is at all unfavourable.

Centuri (Corsica)

Lat. 42° 58′ N
Long. 9° 21′ E

AVAILABLE: Water.

A very small fishing boat harbour but, again, not suitable for the average sized cruising yacht as most of the harbour is shallow. Centuri should not be considered as a port of call except in perfect weather conditions.

Saint Florent (Corsica)

Lat. $42°\ 41'\ N$
Long. $9°\ 18'\ E$

AVAILABLE: Water, fuel, chandlery.

A small but new harbour in a delightful setting, with a beautiful beach around and a background of tree lined hills.

A selection of shops is available only a short walk into the town which was founded by the Genoese in the 15th century and retains an old fashioned elegance.

Saint Florent has a beautiful setting and a new harbour built for yachtsmen, making it a splendid arrival port as an alternative to Calvi.

170   French Mediterranean Harbours

Ile-Rousse (Corsica)

Lat. 42° 39′ N
Long. 8° 56′ E

AVAILABLE: Nothing alongside.

A fairly large and open harbour. Dredging and harbour improvements are taking place (see photo).
The quay to starboard on entry is shared by commercial vessels but stay on this if available; if other yachts are stern-to you will obviously follow suit. The quay ahead is sloping and impracticable. There is plenty of room to anchor in three to four

Reproduced from British Admiralty Chart No. 1126 with the sanction of the Controller H.M. Stationery Office, and of the Hydrographer of the Navy.

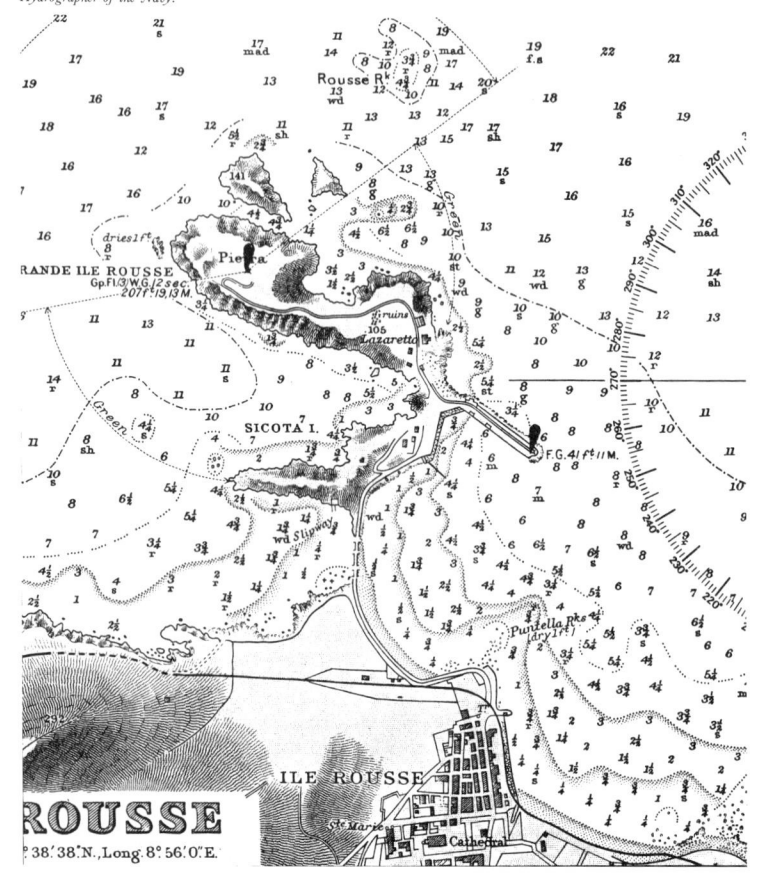

Dredging and harbour improvements seen taking place at Ile Rousse.

fathoms but if the wind is in the east it is most uncomfortable in here.

There are no facilities near the harbour and it is quite a long and dusty walk to the little town of Ile-Rousse; but you should make the effort for it is a charming little place in a quiet fashion.

St. Ambrogio (Corsica)

Lat. 42° 36′ N
Long. 8° 50′ E

AVAILABLE: Water, fuel.

A very small private harbour cum development ashore.

The entry to the harbour is quite narrow and difficult and should not be attempted in unsettled weather.

There is nothing ashore here to tempt the cruising yachtsman.

Index

Agde	70
d'Agde, Cap	68
Ajaccio	158
des Anges, Baie	135
Antibes, Gallice, Port	132
Antibes, Vauban, Port	133
Arles	14
Atalanta	41
Bandol	100
Banyuls	85
Barcarès, Port	76
Bastia	166
Beaulieu	144
Beecham	38
Bonifacio	162
de Bouc, Port	92
Calor Gas	45
Calvi	154
Camargue, Port	60
Canet et Roussillon	78
Cannes	127
Cannes, Pierre Canto, Port	129
Cap Ferrat	142
Cargesse	157
Carnon, Port de	63
Cassis	96
Cats	56
Cavalaire	110
Centuri	160
Cerbére	86
la Ciotat	98
Cogolin, Port de	113
Collioure	82
Communal, Port	149

Cooking	45
Corsica	29, 158
Côte d'Azur	21
Dogs	56
Embiez, Ile des	102
Ferrat, Cap	142
de Fos, Port	92
la Galere, Port	120
Gallice, Port	132
Garavan, Port	150
Girolata	156
Golfe Juan	131
Grande Motte, la	62
Grau-de-Roi	14, 61
Grimaud, Port	115
Hillyard	40
Hire Cars	56
Hyeres	107
Ile-Rousse	170
Languedoc-Roussillon	16, 58
le Lavandou	109
Leucate, Port de	75
Macinaggio	160
Mail	56
de Mandelieu, Port	125
Marseille	94
Measures	57
Menton, Communal, Port	149

Menton, Garavan, Port	150	St. Mandrier	104
Monaco	146	St. Raphael	117
		St. Tropez	111
la Napoule	125	Ste. Maxime	116
Nice	137	Sanary	101
la Nouvelle, Port	15, 74	Seadog	39
		Séte	14, 66
Palavas	65	Shopping Vocabulary	53
Porquerolles	108		
Porto	156	la Tamarissiere	71
Porto-Pollo	160	Telephone	56
Porto-Vecchio	165	Theoule	123
Propriano	161	Toulon	105
Public Holidays	55	Trailers	44
		du Trayas, Port	120
Rague, Port de la	124		
Refrigerators	45	Valras-Plage	72
Rhône	13	Vauban, Port	133
		Vecchio, Porto	167
Sagone	157	Vendres, Port	83
St. Ambrogio	171	Villefranche	139
St. Cyprien	80		
St. Florent	169	Water Heaters	45
St. Jean	142	Weights	57
St. Louis, Port	14, 91		

Carnon Port Camargue
Sète
Gulf of Lions
Leucate
Port Vendres Cerbère

MINORCA

MAJORCA